A Psychoanalytic Stud
of the Wounded Heal

A Psychoanalytic Study of the Wounded Healer uses qualitative research to examine the popular myth that therapists are 'wounded healers'.

Rhona M. Fear presents the life stories of seven well-known psychoanalysts and psychotherapists, including Sigmund Freud, John Bowlby and Patrick Casement. Fear uses grounded theory to analyse her research and categorise her results, focusing closely on experiences including trauma in early life, attachment problems, mental disturbance and resistance to authority figures. The book identifies patterns and common themes in the life stories of these leading figures and explains what this research can tell us about the enduring myth of the wounded healer.

Accessibly written, *A Psychoanalytic Study of the Wounded Healer* will be of great interest to psychoanalysts, psychotherapists, counsellors, and others in the helping professions.

Rhona M. Fear is a psychoanalytic psychotherapist who has spent more than thirty years in private practice in Worcestershire, UK. Following her attainment of a master's degree in counselling and psychotherapy, she proceeded to train in contemporary psychoanalytic theory with the West Midlands Institute of Psychotherapy. She is the author of several books, including *Attachment Theory: Working Towards Learned Security* (Routledge).

A Psychoanalytic Study of the Wounded Healer

Life Stories, Myth and Reality

Rhona M. Fear

Routledge
Taylor & Francis Group

LONDON AND NEW YORK

First published 2023
by Routledge
4 Park Square, Milton Park, Abingdon, Oxon OX14 4RN

and by Routledge
605 Third Avenue, New York, NY 10158

Routledge is an imprint of the Taylor & Francis Group, an informa business

British Library Cataloguing-in-Publication Data
A catalogue record for this book is available from the British Library

ISBN: 978-1-032-32738-9 (hbk)
ISBN: 978-1-032-32736-5 (pbk)
ISBN: 978-1-003-31650-3 (ebk)

DOI: 10.4324/9781003316503

Typeset in Times New Roman
by Apex CoVantage, LLC

It gives me great pleasure to dedicate this book to Dr. Robin Harriott (B.A. Hons., M. Phil., Ph.D.) of Leintwardine who has been kind enough to edit three of my published works. Robin has given incredible attention to detail, and I am in awe of his editorial insights.

Contents

Introduction

It is quite common for counsellors and psychotherapists to think of themselves and others in their profession as 'wounded healers'. Sometimes, this label has a positive connotation – the idea being that therapists themselves have suffered experiences of significant psychological and emotional wounding during their lives prior to taking up this profession and that as a consequence, this 'wounding' enables them to empathise more fully with their patients and clients. However, at other times the term 'a wounded healer' is used in a pejorative manner – implying, I believe, that therapists choose their profession as a direct consequence of their wish to come to terms with their own 'woundedness' and that the career choice is partially made in order that they may experience some sense of personal healing by assisting others. I feel that this may be viewed as unethical by some therapists – and, indeed, some patients. It is generally felt that we as therapists should not seek to work through our own personal difficulties during our work, but rather we should focus fully on providing succour to our clients. Perhaps, however, it is also possible to take the view that if the therapist happens to find her work has a personal healing effect, that this supplementary gain is a legitimate spin-off which she is entitled to receive through her dedicated work as a therapist. One might ask: is it reasonable that therapists, unlike other professions, should only be motivated by pure altruism? Is it not natural that the therapist might hope to answer her own needs as a by-product of helping others? Truthfully, I feel bound to ask – does pure altruism actually exist? Is it not so that the altruist is repaid by a sense of personal satisfaction from having given help to others in their hour of need? It is also possible to believe that each of us, as individuals, is dedicated to put our efforts into a profession that we find personally satisfying and that if we derive some emotional benefit ourselves, this is not proscribed for those who work in all of the caring professions.

I have, for a long time, been fascinated by the idea that many of us in our profession are 'wounded' in some way. As I have outlined, for some this term has negative connotations; for others, the idea has positive connotations attached to it. Within my own psyche, the idea that many therapists could be 'wounded healers' 'chimes' with my own experience in life, and I have heard the echoes of this in many a conversation I have enjoyed with colleagues over the past three decades.

DOI: 10.4324/9781003316503-1

However, I am also well aware that other of my colleagues' struggle with this notion and see it as compromising their integrity in the therapy world as professional, trained therapists.

Consequently, I decided that my plan to write a book on the subject would begin with no specific hypothesis that we either are or are not 'wounded healers'. I took the decision to undertake a piece of qualitative research that would allow the evidence to speak for itself. I am mindful of the fact that although I chose to carry out an enquiry without holding a specific hypothesis, it is virtually impossible for one to completely reduce one's own personal biases so that they have no effect whatsoever. In other words, I am admitting that, for many years, I have thought that it is likely that some of us are attracted to the profession partially by virtue of our own wounds. I am also aware from many years of intensive personal therapy that I regard myself as having been unconsciously drawn to those individuals who appear 'wounded'. This belief, nowadays, is fully conscious. I have attempted to put these inherent biases to one side by devising the research project with which I will shortly familiarise you. I have also kept a reflexive journal throughout my research whilst writing this book. I have aimed, by keeping this journal, to ever hold in mind my own motivational process and to be able to monitor my thoughts, emotions and behaviour as they change and/or become more pronounced. I then used this journal to set my findings in context towards the end of this book.

In trying to decide what research method I should employ, I considered carrying out the research using primary data – that is, by asking a group of individual therapists for their views on the concept of the 'wounded healer' and trying to ascertain whether they had ever characterised themselves as 'wounded'. In order to complete this research, I felt that I would need to carry out semi-structured interviews by asking a few well-conceived open questions about my respondents' personal lives. This would naturally involve engaging with my respondents in an intimate discussion, encouraging them to recount details of their personal life histories and their own thoughts and feelings in considering whether they have a proclivity to class themselves as 'wounded'. I am mindful that psychotherapists and psychoanalysts have, in actuality, a tendency to be very private individuals. This may be partially as a result of being taught the rule of abstinence: that one should refrain from self-disclosure in our consulting rooms – in short, that we should actively avoid the sharing of personal details, problems or dilemmas with patients. However, one might also ask whether some of us choose this particular profession because we are trying in some way to avoid feelings of vulnerability in our daily lives. The argument is somewhat 'chicken or egg'. Do individuals choose this profession because it enables them to gain a sense of connection with their fellow men while at the same time it serves to habitually protect them from voicing their own personal vulnerability? If this hypothesised situation is an accurate reflection of reality, then I was left wondering whether my chosen respondents would be willing to unburden themselves to me in my role of interviewer/researcher. It is true that individual colleagues may assent to take part in the research from a sense of loyalty but then be resentful concerning the sharing of personal details that such a process involved. They may finish the sharing of information by feeling that they had suffered an intrusion into this personal aspect of their lives, and I would not want to incur any ill-feeling. I am mindful that when I was a student at university, we would all agree to take part in each other's research with alacrity for the sake of mutual reciprocity and shared interests. Now, many years after my final qualification, I am not so sure that individuals would be so kindly disposed towards the prospect of providing personal details. As we know all too well, as therapists in our consulting rooms, it takes time for a new patient to feel safe enough with us to disclose what they frequently regard as 'the unspoken secret'. Might my hypothetical participants find that they did not want to share with me the intimate details of their lives, and might I thus only collect answers that were given so as to avoid displaying such vulnerability? Having carried out several 'pilot' interviews informally, I discovered that some respondents did not possess any conscious awareness of the links between their personal history and their eventual choice of profession and thus were not able to answer in a useful format. Others simply avoided giving personal details and did not truly answer the range of questions. In consequence, I decided that the responses might not be particularly helpful in eliciting enlightenment concerning the 'wounded healer' thesis.

Having thought about this dilemma for a number of months, I decided that the use of primary data was impractical given the fact that I also lack a ready supply of respondents as one might have if working in a university or institutional setting. I have been a sole practitioner for more than thirty years, and as you may be aware, it is a lonely path to tread. I was left with the conundrum for several months concerning the form that the research should take. What alternative data might I gather for my research?

As a result of this dilemma, I began to consider the use of secondary data. As I started to become enveloped in the myth of the 'wounded healer', I read a number of therapists' autobiographies. Could I possibly use such texts as my secondary data? Were there enough psychotherapists' autobiographies and biographies in existence? I undertook a literature review of texts and papers that have been published on the subject. My search found a relatively small clutch of literature. Also, it was apparent that the majority of texts referred to therapists of a psychoanalytic theoretical orientation. Perhaps this is not surprising, given that such individuals (like me) love to listen to the gradual unfolding narrative of an individual's life. The idea of writing a text on the concept of the 'wounded healer' among the psychoanalytic community appealed to me. Naturally, if I were only to research the lives of those therapists of a psychoanalytic modality, then my findings might only be applicable in that specific context, thus leaving an opening for further research to be carried out regarding, say, therapists of a humanistic or cognitive-behavioural modality.

After further consideration, I decided to proceed using secondary data. First of all, having questioned whether I could find a sufficient number of autobiographies and biographies, I was pleased to affirm that it was possible, although it is true that as psychoanalysts are relatively private individuals, few have published their autobiography. I was fascinated to find that Karnac (now Routledge) published an autobiography by Patrick Casement (2015), which proved to be a very popular book. Imagine my delight when I found out that Neville Symington (2016) had also recently written an autobiography, also published by Karnac. I finally decided to base my research upon the life stories of seven individuals who have made psychotherapy and analysis their vocation in life.

Next, I needed to give some thought to the research tool that would best answer my cause. Here, my years studying for a masters' degree under the aegis of Professor John McLeod at the University of Keele stood me in good stead. Fortunately, we had studied research methods as they apply to counselling and psychotherapy during the second year of the degree. You may be aware that it was John McLeod who was a founding member of the group that inaugurated the Annual Research Conference held by The British Association of Counselling and Psychotherapy (BACP). He is also the author of a number of books and numerous journal papers on the subject of research. I was fortunate enough to have John as mentor and supervisor for the duration of the year in which I wrote my dissertation. And the practical value of what I had learned over twenty-seven years ago has proven beneficial. Indeed, I remembered that if I employed grounded theory (a research method first introduced by Glaser and Strauss in 1967), one commences the research with a question in mind but without any specific hypothesis. The research process involved in grounded theory enables one to gradually and simultaneously deduce, induce and analyse the data so that one develops a rationale which accounts for the fact that identified categories or themes repeatedly appear throughout the data.

****

But first, a digression regarding another book of mine that was published in 2016. In fact, the subject matter of a previous book and this one are interrelated. This had become clear from my analysis of the research data carried out prior to putting pen to paper. Just as I completed my secondary research into the concept of the 'wounded healer' and had begun to write the Introduction to this book, my second book, *Attachment Theory: Working Towards Learned Security* (Fear, 2017), was published. This book sought to promulgate a new theory that is emerging from John Bowlby's concept of attachment theory. I describe this as 'the theory of learned security'. The book elucidates the way in which it is possible for the relational therapist to help their patients to develop a sense of 'learned security' in the safe haven of the consulting room. My aim in writing that book was to widen and expand the debate among attachment theorists, specifically, to put forward and publicise the way of working clinically that I have evolved during my thirty years in practice. During those years, I elected to specialise in working long term with patients whose wish it was to engage in a prolonged period of therapy and who possess the necessary availability of time, money and motivation to maintain this impetus. Gradually, I came to realise that the underlying motivation to prioritise personal therapy in life is usually derived from the individual suffering a severe developmental deficit or traumatological experience during the early years. This deficit has left such patients with identifiable modes of relating (insecure ambivalent or insecure avoidant, to use Mary Ainsworth's typology) which invariably repeat the pattern of their first original significant relationship with their primary attachment object in childhood. Until they present in therapy and go through an experience of learning through the therapeutic relationship a different, more secure way of relating, there is a tendency to repeat the experience of this type of attachment in their everyday adult life.

This book has been well-received by its audience – in short, whilst this book has the capacity to be of general interest to the community of psychotherapists and counsellors, I believe that it will particularly appeal to those practitioners who tend to practice the tenets of relational psychotherapy, whether or not they are adherents to John Bowlby's attachment theory (Holmes, 1993) or prefer, say, a Kohution approach (Kohut, 1971, 1977, 1984).

It may seem – as I intimated earlier – that I have digressed from the subject matter of the book you are now reading by telling you a little about my book on attachment theory. However, it seems to me from my recent research that the theory of learned security and the concept of the 'wounded healer' are closely related to one another, so I suppose that it is not surprising that I am drawn to the concept of the 'wounded healer', given that the relational world is of such significant interest to me. It was whilst writing the book on learned security and attachment schemas that I began to ponder the knotty and convoluted question of the predominant attachment schemas of the majority of therapists. Having been a member of this profession for three decades, and having undertaken three prolonged qualifications as well as innumerable short courses, I have become conversant with the life histories of quite a number of colleagues and co-participants during experiential exercises. I had not studied the life histories of various well-known therapists from their autobiographical accounts. I began to wonder whether we choose to become therapists and, furthermore, find out that our career choice provides us with a sense of vocation, as a direct consequence of our predominant attachment schemas. Although this thought had already permeated my consciousness, I consciously put the idea on hold whilst I researched the lives of a number of psychoanalysts in order not to make any premature judgements about the factors that may come to light.

In Chapter 12, I have written about the concept of reflexivity – the manner in which, as researchers, we should try to consistently bear in mind what biases and judgements we bring to the table ourselves, and these ideas were noted down in a reflexive journal I kept throughout the writing of this book.

However, I admit quite unapologetically that I have approached this research into the concept of the 'wounded healer' with the bias that I do see the world from a psychoanalytic perspective. It seems only rational that anyone who has an interest in the myth of the 'wounded healer' is very likely to be interested in the protagonists' early life events and the effect of these upon the growing psyche. As has been stated in various texts about research methodology in psychotherapy and counselling, to a certain extent, we each intuitively pre-select the subject we decide to investigate – whether it be to carry out some research project, write a book or present a workshop or seminar. Understandably, we tend to focus upon what interests us and draws our attention. It is for this reason primarily that the researcher needs to investigate and monitor her reflexivity and to make it transparent in any thesis into which she delves. I do remember clearly reading this more than two decades ago in John McLeod book, *Doing Counselling Research* (McLeod, 1993). It is doubtless because of my fascination with each individual's unique life narrative that I developed a career as a psychoanalytic psychotherapist. Taking this into account, it is therefore hardly surprising that whilst writing the book on attachment theory, I began to mull over the myth of the 'wounded healer'. Indeed, is it not so that we, as therapists, are just as much a product of our own early life experience as are our patients?

I soon became aware that one of my close friends who is a psychoanalytic psychotherapist fundamentally dislikes the notion of the wounded healer, finding it irritating. She had given much consideration to her early life during her training analysis and found nothing that indicates that she is a product of woundedness. Partially in consequence of this discussion, I am particularly aware that the myth of the wounded healer may meet with resistance in some quarters. I accept this, just as I accepted that not everyone who looks through the prism of psychoanalysis agrees with John Bowlby's promulgation that environmental failure is as important as, if not more important, than intrapsychic conflict as the cause of neurosis. However, I would surmise that the fact that you have chosen to buy a copy of this book means that you have already given some credence to the concept that many of us are drawn to this profession or others in the caring professions because it is either a way in which we can seek (consciously or unconsciously) to provide a salve for our own wounds or, alternatively, because we have become sensitised to the wounds of others as a result of our own psychological injuries. As I have intimated earlier, it seems to me that if we believe that we take on the responsibilities of this profession in order to provide a salve for our own wounds – it is debatable that there exists something of a moral dilemma. Just as we are counselled to abstain from self-disclosure if it is solely for our own benefit, similarly, is it not therefore unethical for us to enter this profession predominantly with the *express* intention of healing ourselves? I stress the word 'express' advisedly by drawing attention to it in italics. Harding Davies (2004) states in her book that researches the effects of counsellor training upon neophyte counsellors that several participants did admit they at least possessed a dim awareness of their own woundedness and were motivated to undertake personal therapy and participation in awareness groups during training so that they could glean some answers to personal difficulties. This puts yet another perspective upon choice of career: if one chooses a career partially because one is interested in the process of becoming a therapist and feels drawn to the need to enter therapy oneself and process inner feelings in awareness groups, then this appears to me to be a logical and valid choice. One is not cynically exploiting one's patients for personal gain.

I have been interested for many years now in the concept that each of us adheres to a particular type of world view (*weltanschauung*) or vision of reality. I believe our world view develops as the result of an assortment of factors – partly, it results from our inherent genetic characterological and constitutional make-up; partly from the life events that we have experienced; partly as a result of the world view of those who raised us. In the dissertation for my master's degree, I looked at the relationship between an individual counsellor's personal metatheoretical assumptions and his or her choice of theoretical orientation. My hypothesis put forward the argument that if one chooses a theoretical orientation of which the metatheoretical assumptions are at odds with one's own personal metatheoretical underpinnings, then the individual therapist will either leave the profession, change theoretical orientation or suffer the experience of burnout. In short, such an individual would daily be challenged by a severe level of cognitive dissonance. In the research for my dissertation, I chose to investigate the metatheoretical assumptions of individuals by using a typology of visions of reality developed by the literary critic Northrop Frye (1957, 1965). I shall discuss the four differing visions of reality and their philosophical underpinnings in detail in Chapter 3. You will find that this concept of vision of reality or world view becomes relevant to my findings regarding the wounded healer myth in the later chapters of this book and in my discussion of my findings at the conclusion of the book.

A Note on the Nature of Biography

Adam Phillips – the psychoanalyst whose biography of Freud, *Becoming Freud: The Making of a Psychoanalyst* (Phillips, 2014), I found so fascinating – makes a point that I believe deserves mention at this stage. Freud actively discouraged the idea that individuals might seek to write biographies about him. He first wrote to Martha Bernays, his fiancée of four years, in 1885, telling her that he had destroyed all his personal correspondence and letters (apart from hers) with the express intention of making it difficult for all of his biographers (ibid, p. 25). In fact, I find it somewhat grandiose and telling in more ways than one that this man, who at the age of twenty-nine had yet to achieve any notoriety, should be so confident as to think that there would be multiple biographies written about him. Notwithstanding this fact, I want to point out the reasons that Freud felt that biographies never told the truth. Primarily, Freud believed that "nothing in our lives is self-evident, that not even the facts speak for themselves" (ibid, p. 4). He believed that we come to therapy to enable the unspeakable to be spoken. Our neurotic and psychosomatic symptoms have been developed in order to sublimate 'the facts' – in essence, he means that the facts are disguised via the use of defence mechanisms. He stated quite accurately, I think, that many of us do not want to be cured (although we profess to want this more than anything at the outset of therapy). It is for the very reason that we resist the uncovering of the truth that we have developed "a defensive structure". Balint named this feature when the analysand does not lose this defensive structure throughout an analysis as "malignant regression" (Balint, 1968). Indeed, it is to Freud that we owe the inclusion of the word 'defensive' in relation to matters of the psyche. Phillips says that Freud's view of childhood was that it "informed everything but predicted nothing" (ibid, 2014, p. 11). I would agree; my experience as a psychoanalytic psychotherapist has shown that no two individuals who may have suffered a similar experience will have been affected by it in precisely the same way. One may have developed a profound neurosis; the other may seem relatively unaffected until one starts to delve beneath the surface. One person may have found a temporary "solution" (Fear, 2016) by the use of a defensive structure, whilst another may live on with no developed way of dealing with the intrapsychic conflict that is endured. Indeed, it is possible that the way that a neurosis presents is often unique to that individual.

It is certainly possible that two individuals with similar 'facts' in their upbringings may be affected very differently. Take, for example, the early life story of Khalid Masood. Masood purposefully ran his car along the pavement over Westminster Bridge, mowing down pedestrians of many nationalities, and then drove into the grounds of the Palace of Westminster and fatally stabbed a policeman. An article that circulated in the press at the time attributed his state of anomie and alienation from our society to the fact that he was born a black child to a white, Caucasian, seventeen-year-old mother. While it is true that the school photographs provide evidence that his was one single black face amongst many white faces at his school, this is not sufficient reason to presume that he would become liable to a process of radicalisation. My own eldest nephew was born to my unmarried sister, a Caucasian, when she was nineteen. His father is Nigerian, so in consequence, he is of dual heritage, and he attended primary school in England, where he too was one black face amongst many white during the sixties. However, he has gone on to develop a very successful career as an oil and gas engineer in the United States of America, of which we are all rightly extremely proud. He has a lovely wife and two sons whom he loves very much. This is just one further example of the sheer unpredictability regarding the way in which a person will be affected by adverse life events. So much depends upon extraneous factors, interrelationships and one's own characterological makeup and mental state.

It is axiomatic, too, that individuals attend therapy seriously declaring that they want to find a better, more satisfying way of living, but in actuality, they resist the giving up of their neurotic solutions, especially during the early years of therapy. You need only read some of the case studies in my first book, *The Oedipus Complex: Solutions or Resolutions?* (Fear, 2016), to discover that the neurotic solution that the individual client has developed in order to deal with their unresolved Oedipus complex (which I term the 'solution'), may be clung onto by the client for quite some time during the early years of therapy. Resistance and repression are writ large in the consulting room at this stage. However, most individuals gradually acquire the insight to appreciate that their 'solution' has broken down and that a healthier option might be open to them. Admittedly, it is the effect of breakdown that provokes many patients to seek therapy in the first place. With the use of a process that effectively means that the individual remembers, repeats and then works through, in the transference (Freud, 1914), the individual frequently ends the therapy when he or she has achieved a new understanding of his or her internal struggles and worked out (within the therapeutic alliance) a new way of living. In this way, 'resolution' as opposed to 'solution' is reached and celebrated (Fear, 2016).

So, in consequence of more than thirty years in practice, I possess a far more optimistic view of our patients. Whilst complete 'cure' is mostly not achievable – some residue of the neurosis remains, and comes to the fore during times of stress – many of my patients go on to lead a far more productive and healthy way of living which I believe emanates from a prolonged period of their lives in therapy. I may remind you that Freud often saw his patients for only a few months. He worked with Anna Guggenbuhl (Koellreuter, 2016) in therapy from April 1, 1921, to July 14, 1921 – a total of just eighty sessions over a period of four months. We would regard this nowadays as short-term therapy, even though Freud did see his patients six days a week. Once, Freud stated that he analysed a patient for a period of four hours on a walk whilst he was on holiday! We would not now feel that this entitled Freud to the credence that he was given at the time because of the way we now conceive of long-term analytic work. Consequently, is it of any surprise that Freud wrote to his dear friend and mentor, Wilhelm Fleiss (Freud, 1950 [1892–1899]), in the early days of his career, complaining that a lot of his cases were not reaching a satisfactory conclusion? In fact, this was partially the reason that led him to revise his belief that his female hysterical analysands had in fact suffered sexual abuse at the hands of family members as they declared. You will no doubt be familiar with Freud's cataclysmic decision and volte-face that such female patients had suffered sexual relationships in phantasy rather than reality. Part of the reason for his revision was that he was not achieving the anticipated success in the analyses he was carrying out. Is it not likely that the original premise was not in actuality faulty, but lack of success was a result of too short a period in analysis? I have found in my practice that if there is profound disturbance, it takes a prolonged period of time to undo early traumatological events.

I return now to Freud's statement that the facts of our patients' lives do not provide an accurate picture by themselves. In order to maintain the status quo, patients will unconsciously or consciously misrepresent the truth. As Freud said, the facts do not speak for themselves. But is it not the task of the therapist to analyse the facts with which we are presented in the therapeutic hour and to connect what our patient may have said today with a different 'fact' he presented three months ago or five years ago? In other words, we sift through the plethora of facts and opinions put forward during a therapy, and whilst it is perhaps appropriate that we should approach every therapeutic hour "without memory and without desire" (as Bion (1984) cautioned us), nevertheless, it is up to the individual analyst to gradually construct a whole picture of the jigsaw pieces that the patient hands to us, piece by piece, in the process of his or her sessions.

In this way, by constantly approaching what is communicated to me either verbally or through the counter-transference, I employ a process of sifting, analysis and making connections so that I can construct a fairly accurate picture of an individual's life. It is true, as Freud said, that the facts do not speak for themselves, but it is untrue, in my experience, that we cannot eventually, with assiduous endeavour, arrive at an approximation of what we may refer to as 'the narrative truth'. I believe, therefore, that I have approached my research using secondary data in a similar way. Take, for example, Patrick Casement's two books: *Learning From Life* (2006) and *Growing Up? A Journey With Laughter* (2015). The latter is an autobiographical account; the former a partly autobiographical account of different times in his life, though both cover some of the same ground from a differing perspective. Here is an opportunity to sift through what he says. To compare and contrast. To add and subtract. To wonder what he means by a particular statement. I am sure that Patrick Casement, of whom I have always been a sincere admirer (since the publication of his initial book, *On Learning From the Patient* (Casement, 1985), means to tell us the truth. However, I am sure that he would be the first to agree that he too is affected by his own neurosis, pathologies and defensive mechanisms. I would suggest that these are present in his autobiographical accounts as well as in his daily life.

An Overview of the Structure of the Book

Following the introduction, the first chapter informs the reader about the history of the myth of the wounded healer. The roots of the myth lie in shamanism and the idea that Jesus is a wounded healer himself. You may find the Greek myth of Chiron, the wounded centaur, very interesting as well. The concept of the therapist being a 'wounded healer' was initiated by Carl Jung, the Swiss psychoanalyst.

The second chapter concentrates upon the research methodology. I explain the process of grounded theory and the reasons for my decision to use secondary data derived from the narratives of individuals' lives. I also discuss the history of my fascination with the study of narrative.

In Chapter 3, I develop the idea of narrative as a medium by discussing some of the common mechanisms used in narrative to create the required 'narrative tone'. This chapter includes a short description of two concepts that are seminal to this book – attachment theory and world views. It is important that the reader grasps the basic ideas of both of these concepts/theories in order to join me in the voyage of discovery I take through the analyses of the life narratives of the therapists whose lives I have studied. In order to define the differing visions of reality, I have adopted a typology first invented by Northrop Frye. He was a literary critic who studied the differing world views adopted by Shakespeare in his plays. Frye wrote two well-known books on the subject, *An Anatomy of Criticism* (Frye, 1957) and *A Natural Perspective: The Development of Shakespearean Comedy and Romance* (Frye, 1965). He devised a four-part typology: the names he gave to these world views were Romantic, Comic, Ironic and Tragic. I expect that those of you with anything more than a passing interest in Shakespearean drama can recognise that each of these categories of drama is evident in William Shakespeare's plays. In my chapter on narrative tone, I describe the essence of each of the four visions of reality. I use Frye's typology to analyse the life narratives of the seven psychoanalytical therapists whose life stories I have researched.

Chapters 4 to 10 consist of a sequence of seven chapters, each of which is devoted to the life story of a different therapist. I point out how and where the various concepts occur in each person's life story. Research is never really neat; consequently, each person does not provide an absolutely accurate fit in assimilating each of the six themes in their life story.

In Chapter 11, I summarise the various themes which the research informs me are significant factors leading psychoanalytic psychotherapists or psychoanalysts to be drawn to make a career in the world of therapy. You will have seen in the foregoing chapters that these six themes are found to appear repeatedly in almost all of the life stories of the psychoanalysts that I have studied. It was by using these six themes that I eventually reached my conclusions about the veracity of the 'wounded healer' myth. In this chapter, I elucidate these six themes, which together have enabled me to deduce a theory about the reasons that, in actuality, some therapists do become 'wounded healers'.

Chapter 12 focusses upon the necessity that the researcher remains as reflexive as possible. I draw your attention to the root cause of a number of my possible biases. It is not reasonable to expect that we should be bias-free: that would be impossible. It is more a question of being as aware of the propensity to bias, and to take this into account in one's analysis, findings and conclusions.

The book concludes with a chapter summarising the findings of my research and puts forward a number of ways in which it is possible to look beneath the surface at the myth of the 'wounded healer'. I present my own analysis and opinions of the underlying reasons that wounded individuals find their way into careers as healers. In ancient times, myths formed a way of educating the illiterate masses about the way that their world worked. I speak about this at length in my book covering the legend of Oedipus (Fear, 2016). It is my opinion that in Greek civilisation, it was important to disseminate the message to the populace that incest was to be avoided at all costs. The tragedy that befell Oedipus, with the eventual self-blinding of his eyes using Jocasta's brooches and his subsequent exile to an alien kingdom, is but a fairy tale to explain to the illiterate populace the dire pitfalls of incestuous relationships. Fairy tales and fables provided similar moral-message-giving roles. Could it be that the myth of the wounded healer was also publicised to provide us with a warning of its intendent dangers? Certainly, it seems to me that if the therapist enters the therapy world in order, primarily, to provide a salve for his own wounds, there exists a moral and ethical dilemma. Surely, we are taught the virtues of beneficence and non-maleficence – that we should, as Hippocrates stated, never do any harm; in addition, we should always seek to do good.

Can we fully succeed in this if we have primarily taken up the role of healer in order to relieve our own pain?

I have decided in this book that male and female pronouns and possessive pronouns are used interchangeably. 'She' and 'her' are used when writing about psychotherapists, whilst 'he' and 'his' are used when discussing patients. This is to avoid complications, but of course in reality, it is equally accurate that there are male psychotherapists and female patients.

Chapter 1

The Myth of the Wounded Healer

Shamanism

A shaman is a person who is regarded as possessing an ability to gain access to the spiritual world – the world of both benevolent and malevolent spirits. A shaman will enter a trance-like state; sometimes this state is induced by some sort of ritual, such as a dervish dance or some such pattern of rapid movements. In order to be granted the status of a shaman within a given society, it is most likely that the individual has had a period of severe illness (taking the form of some psychological disturbance) at some stage before being awarded the role of shaman in the community in which she lives. During the process of her illness, a trance or a hallucinogenic state will have been experienced. In actuality, this experience of trance during illness is likely to have been dangerous to the individual's health. It may well have occurred during a psychotic episode, when the person has been temporarily out of contact with reality.

In consequence of this experience, it was (and, in some tribal societies, still is) believed that the individual is an intermediary or messenger between the human world and the spirit world. In short, then, what is it precisely that makes a person gain the role of shaman? She is believed to have the capacity and technical ability to achieve 'religious ecstasy'. Shamans are then utilised by their society to treat ailments and illnesses by mending the soul of the sick through contact with the spirit world. It is believed that by treating the soul, the body of the individual will be capable of rectifying any imbalance; a sense of wholeness will be restored. A shaman will also tend to use her trance-like states in order to seek solutions to problems that are affecting the community, just as oracles were consulted in Greek civilisations.

In fact, various oracles were consulted by both Oedipus and his natural parents, and the oracle became a necessary constituent in the Greek legend of Oedipus. Oedipus' birth parents, Laius and Jocasta, king and queen of Thebes, consulted the Oracle at Apollo regarding their expected baby's birth. They were informed, much to their horror, that the child was fated to kill his father and marry his mother. In order to circumvent this, the putative parents decided to have the baby, once born, be abandoned in the mountains and left to perish, tethered to a rock by his feet (the name of Oedipus means 'pierced heel'). In actuality, Oedipus was rescued by a shepherd and taken to Corinth and given to the childless king and queen,

DOI: 10.4324/9781003316503-2

Polybus and Merope. They lovingly raised him as their son without disclosing to him his true parentage. When Oedipus was a young man, he heard the story of his actual heritage during some revelry and went to the oracle and consulted him regarding this story surrounding his destiny (the myth that he was destined to kill his father and marry his mother). The oracle affirmed that this was his destiny. Oedipus did not question his adoptive parents about the accuracy of this story but took the decision to leave Corinth and travel to another kingdom in order to avoid his destiny. Once in a new land, he met a man at a crossroads, who, unbeknown to him, was actually his birth father (Laius) and, in a violent argument, slew him (thus proving the first part of the prophecy). Oedipus proceeded to Thebes, where he found that the city was tyrannised by a sphinx who killed anyone unable to answer his riddle. Oedipus was the first person to successfully answer the riddle of the sphinx. The sphinx dies. The city is so grateful that they decide that Oedipus should marry the recently widowed queen (who in actuality was his birth mother, Jocasta). Thus, the second part of the prophecy comes to reality. We see in this tale that the oracle was consulted upon a number of occasions. Oedipus consulted the oracle on a further occasion by sending a message via his wife's brother when he became suspicious that he had actually played out this tale of incest.

Beliefs and practices have been categorised as 'shamanic' for many centuries. The roots of shamanism are believed to extend back for two millennia. The idea of shamanism has attracted the interest of many scholars from a wide variety of disciplines, including anthropologists, historians, archaeologists, philosophers and psychologists.

Shamans are normally called to their profession by dreams or signs which require an experience of trance, followed by a lengthy period of training. However, it is also believed that shamanic powers can be inherited.

The 'wounded healer' is an archetype for the idea that an individual goes through a shamanic trial or journey. The process is important to the young shaman. She goes through a period of sickness that has the effect of pushing her to the brink of death. This is believed to happen for two reasons:

1   The shaman crosses over into the underworld during her period of sickness. She is then able to return with information and skills that will be of use to her tribe.
2   It is believed that the shaman must have been 'wounded' in some way by sickness and, from this experience, has gained the capacity to understand and treat others' sickness.

Beliefs

Common beliefs that have been identified by Eliade (1972) include the following:

• Spirits exist, and they play important roles in both individuals' lives and human society.

- Spirits can be malevolent or benevolent.
- The shaman is capable of communicating with the spirit world.
- The shaman is capable of treating illness caused by malevolent spirits.
- The shaman can employ trance-like states in order to go on visionary quests, and they are capable of reaching a state of religious ecstasy.
- The shaman evokes animal images as spirit guides, omens and message bearers.
- The shaman can perform other varied forms of divination, such as the throwing of bones or runes. Sometimes, they can foretell future events.

By engaging in their work, shamans are exposed to significant personal risk from the spirit world, from enemy shamans or by reaching the altered state of consciousness that they employ in performing their roles.

I need to make it clear that in using the term 'wounded healer' for psychotherapists and counsellors, I do not imply that any of us have these supernatural powers or enter into altered states of consciousness in the process of our work. I have taken the decision to talk about shamanism in order to trace the roots of the myth of the 'wounded healer'.

Chiron, Centaur of the Greek World

The first creature to be known as a 'wounded healer' was the centaur Chiron. Centaurs are unusual creatures – they have the body of a horse and the head of a man.

Chiron was the son of Philyra and the Titan god Cronus. Cronos became enraptured and obsessed by Philyra, but she rejected his advances because she found him hideous in appearance. He continued to lust after her and eventually raped her. The result of this union was the baby Chiron. Philyra abandoned the infant shortly after his birth, because she could not bear to look at him, as she found him so repulsive. This may have been as a result of his being a centaur; it may have been because he reminded her of the traumatic rape.

Although centaurs have the upper body of a man and the lower body of a horse, Chiron was different. This was indicative that he was of a higher class than the rest because his front legs were human, as was his head. Other differences between Chiron and his brethren were indicated by the fact that he was far more civilised in nature and did not habitually indulge in drinking to excess or behave lustfully.

The story of how Chiron became a teacher and wounded healer runs as follows. He was with Heracles, who was visiting the centaur Pholus in his cave whilst he tried to complete the fourth task in the Labours of Heracles. A number of those present enjoyed supper together, with Chiron present. Heracles called for wine. Pholus opened some sacred wine that he had been given, but unfortunately, the smell attracted some other marauding centaurs. A brawl broke out, and Heracles killed a number of the centaurs with poisoned arrows. Mistakenly, one of Heracles' arrows hit Chiron, piercing him in the ankle. The fact that he was immortal meant that he did not die but lived from that moment on in terrific pain. As a consequence of this pain, he volunteered to renounce his immortality in exchange for Prometheus' freedom as a response to a request by Heracles. Chiron then took up his place on Mount Olympus with the gods.

Before he was wounded in the ankle, Chiron was known as a great teacher. Once he was suffering the pain induced by the poisoned arrow, he became renowned for his wisdom. It is believed that this wisdom evolved as a result of his intense suffering and his attitude towards it – in effect, that he succeeded in transcending the pain. As a result of this, he was known as the original 'wounded healer'. Many beings presented themselves to Chiron in their suffering, and he was able to heal them and talk to them with great wisdom. We will see this concept of 'transcending' in Jung's idea of archetypes and in Viktor Frankl's recommendations.

A Christian Perspective on the Wounded Healer

A fundamental Christian tenet is that Christ died on the cross to bring salvation; to bring everlasting life. The traditional meaning of the word 'salvation' is that of 'saving' or redemption from sin. However, the original Greek word that is normally translated in this way actually has the more complete meaning of 'healing'. This is the Greek SOZO, and the full understanding of this concept, in recent decades, has extended the Christian message and its theology. The traditional image of Christ on the cross is that of a vulnerable, agonized man, suffering with a piercing thorn crown, nailed hands and feet and a deep spear wound in his side. In the Old Testament prophesies of Isaiah, mankind is promised that "by his wounds we are healed". This is repeated as an essential belief in the New Testament in Peter's Second Epistle. Throughout history, therefore, it has only been natural that the Sacrament of the Eucharist, the sharing and distribution of bread and wine, has been an essential act of worship in churches as a powerful imparting of divine Salvation but also as an act of healing. This has often been accepted in an arguably simpleminded or superstitious fashion, often emphasising physical healing. However, healing the mind of memories, of psychological disturbances, has been a powerful ministerial movement in many Christian traditions, in recent years. Notable have been the contributions of Rev. Professor Henri Nouwen, a Dutch Roman Catholic theologian, and Bishop Henry Morris Maddocks, an Anglican.

Jung's Inauguration of the Myth of the Wounded Healer

The term 'wounded healer' was inaugurated by Carl Jung to describe the way in which therapists are able to carry out their roles in the community. It involves the idea that the analyst is compelled to treat patients as a consequence of his own 'wounds'. Research has shown that three-quarters of counsellors and psychotherapists have experienced one or more wounding experiences, and this impacts their choice of career. They become carers for those in emotional and psychic pain.

This 'wounded' state is believed to affect the relationship between therapist and patient in two ways:

- The therapist is consciously aware of his wounds. The wounds are activated in certain situations, especially when the patient has wounds that replicate those of the therapist.
- The wounds of the patient affect the wounds of the therapist. The therapist communicates this effect to the patient, either consciously or unconsciously. This may be via a process of projection or projective identification or through the therapist's counter-transference. Maybe the patient feels that the therapist understands her empathically – to a greater extent, perhaps, than had a previous therapist with no personal experience of woundedness.

Jung said that it is the physician's hurt that gives him the power to heal, but he adds the warning that one can only heal to the extent that the therapist has addressed and worked through his hurts and has consequently been healed (Jung in Stevens, 1994, p. 239; Jung in Dunne, 2015, p. 119).

Jung felt that depth psychology can be potentially dangerous to the therapist, because he is vulnerable to his wounds becoming reactivated by contact with the wounds of the patient. In order to avoid this, he recommended that the therapist have an ongoing relationship with his unconscious in order to avoid identifying with the "healer archetype" and creating an inflated ego – a sense of being better than and superior to his fellow men (as described by Stevens, 1994, p. 239). Jung believed that by withdrawing his projections, the healer could help to activate the powers of the inner healer within the patient. The therapist, in this way, is able to help the patient's willingness to experience feelings that until now were believed by the patient to be too dangerous or powerful to the body to dare to be countenanced or experienced. In this manner, the inner healer of the patient is activated as a result of the wounds of the healer.

Jung drew on the Greek myth of Chiron to create the myth of the 'wounded healer' as used to describe psychotherapists. As already stated, Chiron transcended his own wounds and became a compassionate teacher who, by virtue of his own constant experience of suffering, was able to empathise with his fellow beings and set their recovery in motion. In short, as I have said, Chiron was able to 'transcend' his own suffering.

This concept of 'transcending' will be seen in the life and work of Viktor Frankl. Having suffered enormously for three years in four concentration camps during the Second World War in Germany, he wrote his treatise called *Man's Search for Meaning* (Frankl, 2004) shortly after his release at the end of the war. He invented the Third School of Viennese Psychotherapy – logotherapy – which encapsulates the belief that it is up to man to transcend his owns suffering, however acute, in order to find meaning for his suffering. By transcending his own suffering, the individual distances himself from his suffering and is able to think beyond it. In so doing, the individual is therefore capable of finding meaning for his experience and can then help others to find meaning too.

Christopher Reeve (who was Superman in the films of that name) seems to be an example of an individual in our times who has accomplished this. He became quadriplegic when thrown from a horse during an equestrian event, and until his death in 2004, he became a champion who tirelessly fought for those who suffer infirmity.

Chapter 2

The Research Methodology

Background to the Research Carried Out for This Project

The myth of the 'wounded healer' is a concept which was first applied by Carl Jung to describe the psychological processes that he believed to occur in the professional and personal lives of psychoanalysts in nineteenth-century Europe. It is my guess that he believed the concept of the 'wounded healer' applied universally to all psychotherapists as a direct result of his own personal identification with the notion. It seems to me that the idea was partly borne out of a massive struggle to come to terms with his own identity. A huge part of that identity lay in the understanding of his *raison d'etre*: namely, in the way he discovered that he was devoted (in the form of a quest) to the world of therapy, both in the clinical setting and in the publishing of his ideas around the world. His personal identity was strongly bound up with his role as a therapist even in the early days of the Burgholzli Psychiatric Hospital in Switzerland, where his clinical experience informed the gradual development of his theory of how the psyche functions.

Jung was a complex character, as will be evident in my interpretation of his life story in a later chapter. It is generally understood that Carl Jung suffered a psychotic episode at the Chateau D'Oex during the First World War. He remained ill after his schism with Freud for some years, and his clinical role was often taken by his wife, Emma Jung, who, by this time, had trained as a psychoanalyst.

I am proposing that the concept of the wounded healer was adopted by Jung because it made sense to him at a personal level. It seems that he distinctly envisaged himself as a 'wounded soul'. In this chapter, I do not want to pre-empt the enjoyment that I hope you will derive from learning of Jung's formative years (in Chapter 9).

It seems feasible, therefore, that the psychological traumas during his early years contributed to Jung's self-perception as a 'wounded healer'. He extrapolated this finding by associating it with his knowledge of the early lives of a good number of other therapists. In this way, he analysed that the concept of the 'wounded healer' – which he adopted from the myth of Chiron – applied to a good number of psychoanalysts and psychiatrists of that time. He believed that the term

DOI: 10.4324/9781003316503-3

particularly applied it to those individuals who derived a sense of vocation from their profession. As you are no doubt aware, Jung's theories relied heavily on the concepts of archetypes, myths and images. Thus, the story of Chiron was no doubt a constituent in the construction of his theoretical framework.

However, having discussed a little about Carl Jung and the myth of Chiron (the centaur), you may start to appreciate how the roots of the wounded healer lie in storytelling. It is to the role of storytelling that I turn next.

Storytelling and Storymaking: My Personal Connection With Stories

I have been fascinated personally by the idea of storymaking and storytelling for almost three decades. In the early nineties, I undertook a master's degree in counselling studies at the University of Keele. A part of the course requirements involved the writing of a dissertation by undertaking a piece of research entailing the collection of some primary data (previously unpublished data). I decided to research what motivated individual counsellors to employ a particular theoretical modality. I remain interested in this subject to this day. Intuitively, I felt that this choice was bound up with their life experience and their personal ideological perspective; in short, by their epistemological style. In order to find out more, I became interested in the underlying metatheoretical assumptions of the differing theoretical modalities. I started to wonder if the counsellor in training was unconsciously drawn to a theoretical modality that shared the same underlying assumptions as those that he or she personally partook of in life. Some of the initial findings led me to proffer the additional hypothesis that if a neophyte counsellor blindly chooses a theoretical modality that does not share the same underlying philosophical values as her own personal ones, this would – in the short to medium term – lead either to burnout or to her changing theoretical allegiance or even to her abandoning the profession. The central purpose of the research, however, was to investigate different counsellors' choice of theoretical modality and to see if this matched the underlying metatheoretical assumptions of their own personal philosophy.

At this point, I was faced with the following conundrum: how would I best measure the individual's metatheoretical assumptions – in other words, their vision of reality or world view? I discovered that the literary critic Northrop Frye had devised a typology of visions of reality with particular regard to Shakespearean literature (Frye, 1957, 1965). Having read his first book, *An Anatomy of Criticism* (1957), I decided to adopt his typology of world views in my own research. I discuss these world views in Chapter 3.

I was delighted to find some academic papers in various journals by Shafer (1976) and Messer and Winokur (1980, 1984, 1986) in which these authors had also used Frye's typology to investigate the metatheoretical assumptions underlying each of the main theoretical orientations. Consequently, I realised with incredulity that I would be able to directly compare the neophyte counsellors' world views and their chosen theoretical orientation in order to discover areas of consonance or dissonance.

At this point in planning the style of my research proposal, I was left with one question unanswered. What research tool could I administer to my respondents if I were to be able to analyse their visions of reality? My research tutor, Professor John McLeod (1993), suggested I use narrative analysis. He suggested that I ask my respondents to write a personal story about an event in their lives. It could be about any subject; it could be of any length; but it needed to have a beginning, a middle and an end (a conclusion). I then analysed the stories in terms of the world view taken by the writer.

This method particularly appealed to me because I have always been an avid reader and have loved storytelling since early childhood. By 1995, I had been a counsellor for some six years, and like most counsellors of a psychodynamic orientation, I was fascinated by the wealth and infinite variety of the life narratives that came to be relayed to me in the consulting room. I still remain, to this day, fascinated and intrigued by the fact that no two people share an identical life narrative. Each person's life story is unique and, in fact, is laden with its own associated beliefs and emotions.

I strongly agree with Jeremy Holmes that one of the central aims of therapy is to help the patient to develop a sense of "autobiographical competence" (Holmes, 1993, pp. 122, 182). It is only when a patient is able to devise a coherent, joined-up story of all of their life events that they are in consequence able to appreciate the underlying meaning of the life events that they have encountered and to gain a sense of perspective about their lives. In this way, an autobiography is at heart a creative process. Psychotherapy can usually successfully come to a conclusion when the patient reaches this point.

I have written about this very topic in my book on attachment theory (Fear, 2017, pp. 98–99), so if you are interested to read more, I direct you to this book and also to Jeremy Holmes's book on attachment theory (1993).

The Meaning of Stories

The reason that I am so interested in stories lies in the fact that they are all true, but they are metaphorical mirrors which provide evidence of different facets of ourselves. They tell of truths – but they are invested with 'narrative truth' rather than pure 'historical truth'. Each story reflects how the individual perceives the world and how he makes sense of his experience. We each, in every story told, choose to include certain aspects and omit others (i.e. we employ a process of selective attention). In this way, we are constantly sifting through our life happenings and unconsciously, or maybe sometimes semi-consciously, represent a certain view of life. This is never seen with more acuity than in autobiography. Here, the teller chooses what to talk about and what to omit; he may choose this quite consciously so as to portray a certain view of himself; it may alternatively be a series of intuitive choices that are made quite unconsciously. The actuality may lie somewhere in the middle of these two positions. One might be driven to ask: is an autobiography a work of fiction or non-fiction? It is certainly true that the author, in telling his life story, may well be engaging in the process of searching for his own sense of identity. Writing one's life story is frequently found to encompass a healing element – it has a cathartic effect. As the author, one is also tending to make sense of how and why one's life has taken the course it has; above all, I think that the writer is adding meaning to his or her own existence.

In biography as opposed to autobiography, the narrator of the story holds a certain degree of power in a similar fashion, but she is perhaps more consciously driven. She is at liberty to include certain facts but to omit others that do not tend to 'prove' the message of the life story she is presenting. Again, this may be carried out consciously; however, it may have an unconscious or semi-conscious element.

Certainly, one looks for facts that interest one as an author, and in so doing, one is selectively inattentive to other aspects of the life of the person about whom one is writing. Even in stressing here the difference between conscious and unconscious process, I am creating a bias in the analysis of the data because of my psychoanalytic theoretical orientation and belief system.

It is partly for this reason – that each of us discloses certain facts about ourselves by our choice of data and 'fact' – that I decided to carry out the research for this book using published biography and autobiography regarding psychoanalytic therapists. I have chosen on this occasion to use secondary data (i.e. already-published material, not material gathered specifically for research purposes) for a number of reasons. First of all, it represents a choice with a practical rationale. The data is readily available. Secondly, each of the writers (be they writing autobiography or biography) will no doubt have differing and unique motivations in setting about the subjects they choose to study. This effectively means that some aspects of inherent bias are minimised by the variety of motivations of the authors. It is equally accurate to note, however, that I have introduced a bias into the sample by choosing only subjects who take an analytic orientation. Consequently, I understand that my findings can only be strictly applied to therapists of a psychoanalytic or psychodynamic modality. However, I am quite happy with this because I suspect that the individuals who are most interested in this subject and are likely to give credibility to the thesis of the wounded healer tend to be of a psychoanalytic or psychodynamic orientation. It is worth remembering that it is these individual therapists who are primarily fascinated by the relationship between the past and the present.

I want to move on at this juncture to a discussion about the structure of story-making. Story is such a central element of this book – as the story of wounded healers – both in terms of the individual life stories of certain personalities and as the modus operandi for carrying out the research for this book.

Different Storymaking

There are the following groups of storymaking:

'Home stories': These are the stories that we tell about ourselves, to other people. Our story may be told in the course of conversation, to while away a cold winter evening, to spread the word to others about the way one has lived one's life (autobiography) or to tell others about a personage that one deems to be significant (biography). Some 'home stories' are personal myths: they are "a sacred story that embodies personal truth" as Dan McAdams states in a fascinating book, *The Stories We Live By* (McAdams, 1993, p. 34). The autobiographies and biographies that I have employed in my research are home stories – they are written to tell stories about particular individuals' lives.

'Teaching stories': These stories are split into a number of sectors:

- Myths
- Legends
- Folk tales
- Fairy tales

All the stories listed tend to contain a message; historically, they were, in effect, ways of teaching what was, in the past, a largely illiterate population about the evils of the world; about norms, mores and values; about lessons that it is wise to imbibe and remember; about 'what makes a person tick'. Some stories, such as fairy stories, were also primarily for the purpose of entertainment, but none the less, they often sought to instruct the infantile listener at the same time. Fables and myths, similarly, were purposefully aimed to help the reader increase his understanding of the world and its social mores, norms and values.

In 2016, Karnac published a book I had written on the subject of the Oedipus complex (Fear, 2016). This in itself is a legend, a myth. It first drew my interest when I attended a workshop led by Michael Jacobs on his reading of Shakespeare's play, *Hamlet*. He highlighted how it could be interpreted as a story of oedipal conflict. The myth of the Oedipus complex has been invented and used for centuries in order to tell the public that no good will come from incestuous relationships – that only crisis and tragedy result if one ignores the timely warnings.

The Oedipus complex is a narrative; the case studies in my book are narratives of a different kind, evidencing the different ways in which an Oedipus complex can manifest in a person's life. I noticed with interest, a year later, that Karnac had published another book on the Oedipus complex by Zepf and Zepf (2016). This book, I believe, turns the accepted version of the Oedipus complex on its head and puts forward the idea that the Oedipus complex is really the story of rivalry between the parents: this is played out in the family by each trying to win the child's love most profoundly. Once again, this book tells another different story.

Story Structure

Stories tend to have a particular structure. It has a structure that even little children, such as three-year-olds, learn to recognise and internalise. Appreciating this, the young child may well be able to differentiate a set of instructions or a journey plan from a story: they may not be able to describe or name the particular structure but they know that lists, for example, do not formulate a story.

A story will have human or anthropomorphic characters. It usually begins with an initiating event, which motivates the central character to attempt to do something. As a result, there is a consequence, to which there is often a reaction. Finally, the story ends with a denouement (a solution to the initiating event). Thus, you will now see why I gave the particular directions to my respondents.

Methodology Chosen in Preparation of This Book

I imagine by now, you will appreciate my lifelong fascination with story. Encouraged by my research supervisor at Keele University, I chose to collect my data by asking each of my respondents to write a story. I can readily admit that I found these stories both fascinating and endearing. There was a promise to maintain confidentiality and to employ anonymity in the research findings. The respondents, in their choice of subject and emphasis upon certain facets of their tale and in their use of narrative tone (see next chapter for details of this), told me so much about each of them as individuals.

This experience has stood me in good stead. As a result of this piece of research and later primary research carried out using workshop students as my sample population, I proceeded to write and publish a number of papers in various journals and chapters in edited textbooks (Fear and Woolfe, 1996, 1999, 2000; Fear, 2004). It was in this way that I commenced my career as a writer.

There then followed some years in which I focussed mainly upon my work as a clinician. However, a few years ago, I once again became predisposed towards serious writing. Having attended the seminar by Michael Jacobs on 'Hamlet on the Couch', I began to connect the ideas he put forward with my own clinical work and gradually devised the plan for a book on the subject of the Oedipus complex (Fear, 2016).

I had always held a belief that many of the texts that one is encouraged or set to read whilst one is in training psychoanalytically are very dense and convoluted in their style. They lack accessibility; they are aimed, in my opinion, at a readership of therapists who are accustomed to the concepts and ideas in the book and who are already in touch with the subject matter. This made me, as a student, sometimes cast away a book in dismay, hoping to read it sometime later when my theoretical knowledge had improved. Occasionally, this day actually dawned; more often, the opportunity never presented itself again. In consequence, the insight into that particular subject matter was never gained. It was as a result of this that I determined to write an academic text purposefully written in an accessible style so that the less well-versed clinician will be able to assimilate the concepts. Feeling that this idea was underlain with some sound logic, I determined to write a text about the Oedipus complex – its various theories and the way we find that it presents in our consulting rooms in the intrapsychic lives of our clients. My book, *The Oedipus Complex: Solution or Resolution?* (2016), came to fruition.

We now move on in time to the summer of 2017: I had almost finished writing two more books by then. Mulling over what concepts were catching my interest at the present time, I started to ponder the myth of the 'wounded healer'. I wondered whether the 'wounded healer' is merely a truism, and if so, why is this the case? I certainly reckon that one's capacity for empathy emanates from the experience of difficulties in one's own life.

I also question the ethicality whether a therapist should use one's experience of providing therapy in order to provide a salve for her own wounds. I could find evidence in Harding Davies's (2004) book that quite a number of neophyte counsellor contributors to her book were aware of their own wounds when they first decided to train as therapists. But does this necessarily mean that they intended to find a solution to their wounds by administering therapy to others? Some counsellors mention, for example, that they believed that the training to become a counsellor would help them to work through and gain understanding about their wounds. I am sure that they will have discovered during the process of training that this does occur in some ways. There are, in fact, opportunities to work on personal wounds if one elects to enter personal therapy during one's training. Perhaps in a less structured way, there are also opportunities to air and work on personal problems and conundrums when one enters into the fray of the *de rigueur* personal development groups (also sometimes called awareness groups or encounter groups). I have no ethical objection to making use of these possible loci so that one can work on personal issues. I am a faithful advocate of personal therapy for all of us as clinicians, both whilst in training and beyond. My view is that we should all undergo the experience of being on the other side of the fence – in other words, we should know just how vulnerable it feels to be a patient, presenting one's inner fears and secrets to a therapist with whom one is not familiar at first meeting. It takes courage of immense proportions. I also believe that most of us will encounter times when we need to discuss personal issues in our own therapy. Indeed, some issues may arise as a consequence of patient material presented in the consulting room. At times, we may be aware that our counter-transference is 'getting under our skin' to some extent. It may well be that on personal reflection, we recognise that some of our patients' material may be related to some personal issue for us.

All of the above discussions touch on ways in which it is personally viable that we ourselves, as individuals, are wounded in some way and may seek to gain succour for those wounds. If we can use our own experiences to help others in similar circumstances, then so much the better. However, what if one is predisposed to use the clinical sessions that one offers to patients as opportunities to process one's own emotions? Might this not be classed as inherently unethical? Is one entitled to use someone else's sessions to benefit oneself? Also, is there not a distinct possibility that if one suffers from such wounds that are as yet unaddressed, this will influence and maybe confuse the counter-transference? Thus, I am strongly of the opinion that woundedness needs to be addressed and worked upon by individuals prior to their becoming therapists and also, at times, during their careers as therapists. This is, indeed, one of the rationales that underlie the dictum that psychoanalytic therapists should themselves undergo intensive therapy (training analyses) throughout their time in training. Furthermore, we are encouraged by our professional organisations and by colleagues to undergo further therapy when an issue raised by one of our patients impinges upon our own psyche.

Why Have I Chosen to Use Narrative in the Research for This Project?

I have chosen to use secondary data in order to research the concept of the therapist being a wounded healer. I felt that secondary data is readily available; at a practical level, it did not require me to source participants. As I have mentioned earlier, the random authorship of the books I have used means that bias is reduced – I am not making use of data that has been gathered with a single purpose. No one individual dominates the writing of these books; I have assumed that different authors will hold differing world views. I have chosen to use seven autobiographies and fifteen other texts. Ideally, I might have preferred to use more autobiographies, but in fact, very few psychoanalysts have published autobiographies. It seems to me understandable that these habitual masters of the art of abstention are reluctant to generously disclose details of their own life histories. However, in order to address the issue of bias, in the case of the autobiographies (by Neville Symington, Patrick Casement and Viktor Frankl), I have used as references two books by each individual. When taking into account the need to reduce bias, I feel that the use of biography rather than autobiography may actually minimise bias rather more effectively. Each author no doubt has a slightly or maybe even vastly differing perspective and motivation in writing about a chosen individual.

I tended to believe that as I am analysing the life stories of differing individuals in order to decide whether they fit the category of 'wounded healer', my choice to analyse the data using that very medium – stories – seems particularly appropriate.

Method of Analysis for This Research: The Use of Grounded Theory

Grounded theory was first introduced by Barney Glaser and Anselm Strauss (1967), and initially, it was known as 'the constant comparative method' in a book entitled *Awareness of Dying* (Glaser, 1967). In Glaser and Strauss's joint book later that year, *The Discovery of Grounded Theory* (1967), the name of the research method was changed to grounded theory. The reason for this name will become clear as I talk about the process involved in the analysis of the data. Essentially, the theory that one constructs is 'grounded' in the data.

Grounded theory actually takes an opposite approach to that taken by most social science research. Most social science research until then had followed the positivist tradition. In the positivist paradigm, the researcher is choosing to test an a priori hypothesis. This theory may have been developed by the individual researcher (e.g. as it was in my master's degree dissertation), or it may be an already-perceived, proven 'fact' that is currently circulating in academic circles. For example, many researchers have carried out follow-up research regarding Mary Ainsworth's Strange Situation test regarding attachment schema. They are questioning whether the primary data that they gather supports or refutes Mary Ainsworth's original findings about how infants with differing attachment schemas react to separation from their attachment object. Research is completed by carrying out replications of her Strange Situation test (Ainsworth et al., 1978; Fear, 2016, p. 28).

By contrast, the researcher using the grounded theory method begins with just a question or maybe even by simply gathering a quantity of qualitative data and observing what emerges. As researchers start to review the first set of data, they start to identify ideas that are repeated: concepts or/and elements that come to the fore. As the researcher works through the data, these ideas are tagged with codes (i.e. the use of different alphabetical designations that apply to the recurrence of a specific idea). The researcher then takes another set of data to study, and proceeds to analyse this in the same way. The second, third and subsequent collections of data are examined in order to ascertain whether the same codes repeat or whether there is a lack of consistency about certain codes. The codes are subject to constant review, and it is then discovered that some of the codes are connected to each other in that they represent associated aspects of an idea that is common to a number of codes. It is possible then to start to group the codes into subcategories. Categories are then devised as consisting of a group of subcategories made up of concepts that have meaning links. The researcher then analyses that the various categories link together into a coherent whole, and at this point, she is able to begin to formulate a whole new theory. Generally, some categories take precedence in the theory making over others. This occurs during the analysis of the data. Different sources of data are used until there is a level of saturation, i.e. no new codes emerge.

Grounded theory was first developed by Glaser when he collected data about dying patients in a hospital. In consequence, he wrote a book entitled *Awareness of Dying* (Glaser, 1967).

One of the main purposes of the 1967 book was to help to legitimise qualitative research. In the 1960s, quantitative research had taken precedence as the primary agreed research method in social science. The use of quantitative data dominated the research paradigm. Qualitative research, on the other hand, tended to lack credibility. It was not seen as providing data that was open to verification. Glaser has since stated that the original 1967 book which first used the term 'grounded theory' (Glaser and Strauss, 1967) mistakenly gave the impression that the process of verification was not important in grounded theory. Conversely, verification of the research is now deemed to be of great importance in grounded theory.

Grounded theory follows these steps:

1   Text is coded, chunk by chunk. Separate codes are used to describe different aspects of the same element. Next, codes are combined to form subcategories, and these merge into categories as one analyses the ideas. This is done by the researcher using a process of deduction, induction and analysis so as to link together the subcategories at a higher level of abstraction. These categories are named at this stage. Glaser (1967) stresses that data collecting, coding and analysis are carried out simultaneously and in relation to each other. They are not approached as different stages of the research process. Having worked on the first piece of data (in my case, an autobiography), the researcher next applies herself to another chunk of text (in my case, another biography or autobiography), and the process is repeated. One is searching for patterns and concepts that reappear time and again; conversely, one also abandons some codes that do not reappear in other chunks of text. According to Strauss and Corbin (1990), this is known as open coding. According to Charmaz (2006), this is initial coding.

2   More coding is then carried out, and examples are noted down in detail. One considers how the concepts link together, and by this process, one starts to create categories.

3   The process of memoing comes next: this involves making field notes about the concepts. I carried out this stage by using divided pieces of A4 pages as I reviewed the data so that I would be able to return to examples of concepts and categories and have notes about my analysis of the data. It is quite an intricate process, and I stress that it is important not to miss this stage of the data analysis; if it is omitted, a lot of detailed examples can be lost forever.

4   The memoing stage is followed by a process of integration, refinement and writing up. The researcher engages in a systematic, synthesised process of induction, deduction and verification.

The narrative of the different books about psychoanalysts and psychoanalytic psychotherapists in the later chapters of this book focus mainly upon the integration and refinement of the theories concerning whether the myth of the wounded healer is verified, and if so, what categories have been found by the analysis of the data to recur time and again. By the use of these categories together, one can deduce a theory about (firstly) the reason that healers may have become wounded and (secondly) found their way into a career in psychotherapy.

Conclusion

I have used a relatively straightforward approach to grounded theory in the research which is directed to determine ideas about 'wounded healers'. I have attempted to systematically devise ever-more-precise codes and then group these into concepts because of their phenomenological links. Categories have then become apparent to me via a process of deduction. In this way, the data has been analysed. I carried out the initial coding and concept making by studying two texts by Patrick Casement about his life. I then took my next chunk of data – Neville Symington's two autobiographies – and found that many of the codes and concepts reappeared. Several codes in particular were not replicated in other data – they appeared in the Casement data but did not seem to recur in following chunks of data. I therefore decided to dismiss such codes. Gradually, as I worked my way through the biographies and autobiographies, I found that the same codes and categories occurred time and again. By a process of synthesising the categories into a whole, I devised a theory about how facets of their lives lead to the majority of therapists becoming wounded. The theory also covers the notion that some people choose 'to make use of these wounds' by following a career in psychoanalytic psychotherapy or psychoanalysis, whereas others have different motivations, and life leads them on different career paths.

Chapter 3

The Narrative Tone of Stories
Attachment Schemas and World View

Narrative Tone: An Introduction

On the day that the baby is born, he has no sense of identity. Nor does he have any idea about how the world works, what he may gain from life or how other individuals will interact with him. Hopefully, as he starts to mature, he will have an expectation that the world is kind and welcoming and that his attachment objects are helpful, providing emotional security, warmth and affectionate love. This is likely to occur only if he actually experiences the provision of this behaviour from those on whom he is dependent and with whom he is intimate. However, tragically, there is almost an equal possibility that he may grow to believe that he lives in a hostile world, possibly as a consequence of his intimates' display of aggressive and rejecting behaviour towards him, along with a lack of positive emotional affect.

During the first three years of life, we are each of us effectively collecting evidence for the vision of reality or world view that we, in our later years, tend to anticipate and construct regarding those whom we encounter. These early experiences will colour our everyday actions and, above all, our attachment schema and our world view.

We all tend to introject the narrative tone of a story by the references made to positive or negative attachments; we also imbibe, in a (partially) unconscious manner, the world view that the author portrays in his writing. This world view, more often than not, encompasses the way that the author personally views the world, or it may be consciously manufactured by the writer in order to portray a certain view of the world that is consonant with the story he or she is weaving. This is true in both fiction and non-fiction. I note in this way that Jilly Cooper's novels about the equestrian racing world focus upon status, prestige and the acquisition of external accoutrements. Whilst the main protagonist, Rupert Campbell-Black, is narcissistically self-involved, we are fascinated to some extent by his charm and the fact that "he bestrides the racing world like a colossus" (Cooper, 2016). Cooper is purposefully promulgating a world view of which the glittery heights appeal to many who thus achieve wish fulfilment vicariously. This is not to say that Cooper does, indeed, inhabit such a world herself. Similarly, to use

DOI: 10.4324/9781003316503-4

the example of a textbook such as *John Bowlby and Attachment Theory* (Holmes, 1993), Jeremy Holmes writes in a reliable, comforting and measured manner that typifies the secure schema of sound relationships which he espouses and to which so many of us wish we could personally relate.

Thus, the attachment style that the author puts forward and his intuitive world view are both worth evaluating and analysing in any narrative – be it non-fiction or fiction. These schemas are central to the narrative tone of the story being told.

I am going to talk next about attachment schemas, because firstly, they are a constituent of most stories, and secondly, they are central to the research and the findings in this book. I shall move on at a later point in this chapter to an exposition of differing world views.

Attachment Schemas

John Bowlby was the father of attachment theory. He is believed to have told Mary Ainsworth (the co-founder of attachment theory) that the idea of attachment as a spatial theory came to him "in a flash" as he was intent upon reading about the behaviour of goslings of greylag geese. He was referring to a study carried out by ethnographer Konrad Lorenz (1937). Lorenz carried out seminal research that revealed the reality that for a specific, discrete period of time during their youth, goslings are subject to what Lorenz termed 'imprinting'. This effectively means that a gosling will attach itself, emotionally and physically (in terms of maintaining proximity), to any moving object that is placed before it during this developmental stage. Lorenz went on to prove that goslings would attach themselves to a human being such as himself or even (incredibly) to a moving cardboard box.

Bowlby realised as a result of reading this research and watching the process of 'imprinting' that attachment is primarily a spatial theory. It relies upon the child seeking, finding and maintaining proximity to his caregiver. If the caretaker is reliably available and ever kindly motivated towards him, he will begin to develop a secure attachment schema. However, attachment is in fact about far more than Bowlby appreciated in his moment of enlightenment. Secure attachment is not only dependent upon the physical proximity of the caregiver but also highly dependent upon the emotional availability of the caregiver. For example, Mother may be physically present, but if, for instance, she is sunk in a deep depressive illness, her child will not be able to bond with her securely. Mother effectively needs to be emotionally "attuned" (Stern, 1985) and responsive to the young one and, above all, to be reliable in her response. It is no good to be warm, welcoming and comforting one day but rejecting and emotionally cold on another day. Reliability in terms of timing and availability is key, as are the maintenance of consistent boundaries that do not vacillate from day to day or hour to hour. If these boundaries are put in place, they are far from being 'cruel', as so many people perceive, but they actually enable the child to feel safe and secure. This is not to say that one should never display irritation or anger towards the child, but the caregiver needs to be able to display her anger in a measured way, never showing wanton aggression or sadism.

Bowlby and Ainsworth developed a three-part typology of attachment styles. In later decades, whilst carrying our further research, Main and Goldwyn (1984) and Main and Solomon (1990) added a fourth style of relating to this typology. The four-part typology is described below, in relation to the child's reaction to separation from the caregiver:

> *Secure Attachment:* In this instance, the child will not be unduly upset when Mother is absent and will settle quickly and easily when she returns. He will greet Mother happily when she returns, displaying pleasure in her company, and will soon resume contented play. This is a function of the fact that he is sure that Mother will be available to him, both physically and emotionally, whenever he needs her. As he grows up, he will gradually learn the joys of delayed gratification (i.e. that he may not always get his needs met immediately, but help will in fact be at hand within a reasonable space of time).

Sixty-six percent of the population are fortunate enough to be securely attached. (Statistics provided by Van Ijzendoorn and Sagi-Schwartz, 2008).

> *Insecure Ambivalent Attachment:* In this mode of attachment, the youngster is likely to be very upset when Mother leaves the room, and it is hard for anyone to be able to adequately pacify him. When Mother returns, the child is likely to display resentment and an ambivalence towards Mother – both wanting her and rejecting her at one and the same time.

This is because the child is not sure in life generally that Mother will be available, emotionally or physically, when he needs her. This is likely to be as a result of Mother having been unreliably responsive, either physically or emotionally or in both modes. Mother may be suffering from mood swings – sometimes being welcoming, placid and kind; at others, she may be rejecting, angry and dismissive. It is the quality of the interaction that is important rather than the quantity. It is not uncommon for the insecure child to develop psychosomatic illnesses as a result of his learning that at times of illness, he receives more avid attention from his attachment figure.

Eight percent of children suffer from insecure ambivalent attachment schema.

> *Insecure Avoidant Attachment:* Children with this mode of attachment will tend to ignore Mother when separated from her and again ignore her on her return. They will neither engage in eye contact nor will they tend to search for proximity to Mother. They play with their own toys but in a rather distracted manner, because in fact they are intent upon keeping a watchful eye on Mother from a wary distance.

This is as a result of the child actually being very unsure that Mother will ever give him the emotional care that he craves. He may also feel quite uncertain that Mother will even return after a period of absence. The child will tend to display aggressive outbursts and finds it difficult to make and keep relationships with peers or adults. He tends to keep a distance, emotionally and physically, from all those with whom he comes into contact.

It is quite possible that Mother may be suffering from her own problems and is preoccupied by environmental circumstance (e.g. her own depressive illness, social deprivation, being subject to domestic abuse or drug or alcohol abuse issues within the family).

In consequence, the child is likely to grow up with the following attachment schema, as described by Bowlby so poignantly: never again to dare to risk giving oneself fully to another person, because it was so painful to be rejected that he or she has resolved never to risk this again (Bowlby, 1944, p. 57).

Twenty-six percent of children have an insecure avoidant attachment style.

> *Insecure Disorganised Attachment:* This attachment style was originally thought to be very unusual. It was believed to present only when patients were seen in psychiatric settings in which Mother or Father had significant mental health difficulties or problems with addiction to drugs or alcohol. More recently, it is thought that this behaviour is actually more common, especially among demographic groups in which the family system is under severe psychological strain or trauma. In such populations, the percentage can rise to 70% of a particular sample population (Van IJzendoorn and Sagi-Schwartz, 2008).

However, it is felt that this percentage in the wider community generally only accounts for 0.1% to 1% of the entire population.

The insecure disorganised child will evidence some stereotypical behaviours: for example, head-banging; 'freezing'; alternatively coming towards Mother and then veering off at the last moment. The child finds it very difficult to make or keep relationships with any other children or indeed, any adults. There are frequent displays of aggression toward others. There are often associated attention deficit problems and behavioural problems identified by the school. Mother is generally unable to calm the child when he is distressed. The child exhibits little motivation to explore in mother's presence.

It will be useful to be conversant with these attachment styles in the narratives that follow later in the book, when we analyse the life scripts of the various analytic therapists whose lives I have chosen to research.

We will find that those to whom a 'wounded healer' label applies have generally learned a less-than-optimal attachment style: either insecure ambivalent or insecure avoidant. We will see in the stories that follow that one of the dominant themes discovered in the research is actually the presence of difficulties of attachment during childhood and adolescence. The root of this difficulty can usually be seen in the individual's family of origin.

World View or Vision of Reality

An individual's world view can be deduced from the way in which he sees the world around him. I found that the capacity to define a person's individual world view was a very important category that I noted in my analysis of the data provided by the biographies and autobiographies that I have utilised in my research. I found, in fact, that 'wounded healers' have tended to imbibe either a Tragic or Ironic vision of reality: these world views both tend to have a relatively pessimistic orientation towards the world.

In order to be able to define the particular vision of reality of the individuals whose life stories I have used in my research, I needed to adopt a defined typology. It seemed natural, given my academic experience (namely my use of Frye's visions of reality in the research for my master's dissertation), that I use this typology again. I refer to the visions of reality (*weltanschauung*, which, translated means 'world view') that were devised by Northrop Frye (1957, 1965). He devised these schemas from the reading of Shakespearean literature in order to attempt to take a more scientific approach to literature rather than relying solely upon his intuition. The names of the four visions are as follows: Tragic, Ironic, Romantic and Comic.

Quite a number of psychoanalytical researchers later used Frye's visions of reality and applied them to the metatheoretical assumptions that can be seen to underlie the four differing main categories of theoretical modality utilised in counselling and psychotherapy. Messer and Winokur (1980, 1984, 1986) and Roy Shafer (1976) wrote a number of papers in journals and books which concentrate upon the visions of reality found in the four main types of theoretical orientation: psychodynamic, humanistic, cognitive-behavioural and integrative. These academics became involved in a study of these metatheoretical assumptions in order to carry out investigations into the viability of theoretical integration. Namely, they were intent upon addressing the issue that there is an obstacle to integration because differing theoretical modalities have competing underlying metatheoretical assumptions that are at odds with one another. This debate widened to investigate the manner in which therapists selected the theoretical orientation they decided best suited them. It was thought that therapists' selection of theoretical orientation was a result of both unconscious and conscious processes.

In what follows, I will present a synopsis of the way in which each of these visions of reality vary in their epistemological style (philosophical stance). Before I begin, I would just like to make it clear that the nomenclature of these world views is in no way pejorative. It is sometimes mistakenly believed that the term 'comic' is used to mean it is an "amusing" approach and that the implication is that the cognitive-behavioural style of counselling should not be regarded as a serious modality. Similarly, the name 'ironic view' could imply that this approach has a cynical component, because the word 'ironic' suggests a wry response to happenings in life. In fact, the names given to each of these visions are not value laden.

The Romantic Vision of Reality

If one is prone to take the Romantic perspective, life is seen as an adventure or journey. The individual takes part in a quest in which he believes it is possible that he will achieve whatever he sets out to do. It is essentially a hopeful, very optimistic vision of life. As White says, it is about the triumph of good over evil, of virtue over vice, of light over darkness (White, 1973, p. 9; quoted in Messer and Winokur, 1986, p. 116), and as Viktor Frankl says, the hope is that the individual is able to transcend his personal suffering through his love for another or his belief that it is his destiny to achieve a certain thing (Frankl, 2004). It represents a view of the world as most of us would wish it to be rather than as we disappointedly discover it to be. Mystery, a sense of a quest carried out by a hero and fusion with some higher power are all aspects that are stressed. The quest ends, after struggle, with the hero's exaltation. There is a sense of persistent nostalgia, and in some respects, this world view is quite childlike and simplistic. The 'hero' is definitely deemed to be capable of self-actualisation; in short, he is seen as capable of achieving whatever he determines.

As I suspect you will have surmised from this description, this world view is held (wholly or partly) by therapists of a humanistic persuasion. The process of self-actualisation is key to this theoretical orientation. Dreams, fantasies, metaphor, intuition and imagery are all stressed. The locus of responsibility and locus of control of the individual are internal – the individual is envisaged as a free agent; he is capable of achieving whatever he sets his mind to accomplish. This view stresses agency rather than external, structural determinants – free will reigns, and there is little recognition of constraints. Carl Rogers stressed the positives in life and focussed particularly upon whatever it was that his client wanted to achieve. If you watch the video of Carl Rogers carrying out a counselling session with Gloria (Shostrum, 1964) in the well-known film detailing the different stances of Carl Rogers, Albert Ellis and Fritz Perls, you will easily perceive that which is being stressed here.

The psychoanalytic orientation has elements of the Romantic vision of reality according to Shafer (1976, pp. 32–33). It is accurate to say that the analysand initially determines to pursue a quest to recover a lost golden age. Freud, in *Analysis Terminable and Interminable* (Freud, 1937), stresses the way patients wish to achieve this, especially at the outset of treatment. For some individuals, this wish remains with them throughout therapy and is believed to be achievable. Freud pointed out the way that analysands tend to rue the fact that they had not been able to fuse with the breast-mother; they regret that their attachment has not been secure and/or has been complicated by adverse life events (such as Mother suffering from depression, as described by Andre Green in *Narcissisme de Vie.*

Narcissisme de Mort (1983)). However, Freud actually espoused the notion that 'cure' is not achievable – the best that therapy can realistically achieve is to convert hysterical misery into ordinary human unhappiness (to paraphrase Freud).

In fact, in terms of the Romantic vision, the heroic fulfilment of tasks is seen to occur as the patient "remembers, repeats and works through" (Freud, 1914) his intolerable anxieties, guilt, yearning and despair in the transference rather than in actuality being able to achieve a totally happy outcome. In this way, the quest is eventually envisaged as encompassing the search for meaning rather than as a perilous journey leading to a golden land. We shall see how an individual may search for this sense of meaning acutely in the description of Viktor Frankl's life. He was, amazingly, able to find meaning for intense levels of suffering; namely, the suffering which he and many others had experienced in the concentration camps of Hitler's Germany.

The Comic Vision of Reality

The person who holds a Comic vision of reality consistently believes in unqualified hopefulness. It is accepted that one does indeed encounter dilemmas and obstacles in one's life, but there is a certainty that every obstacle or evil doing can be overcome if one maintains good intentions. Loss is acknowledged, but it is believed that every loss can be made good; every suffering, however intense, can be relieved.

The Comic vision stresses and focusses upon the external events and situations that seek to 'undo' us at times in our lives, and it counteracts negativity by employing what is now known as the power of positive thinking. There may be hard times, but we are seen to be capable of surmounting them if we take on a positive attitude. You will no doubt recognise the attitude and beliefs of the cognitive behavioural counsellor and, indeed, the rationale of many psychologists who work within a CBT format. I would add, however, that this attitude of CBT counsellors appears to have undergone some amelioration in recent years, as they have come to acknowledge adversity and the immoveable nature of some obstacles (as in acceptance and commitment therapy (ACT)).

Laughter and gaiety are not considered endemic in this vision of reality, whereas worldly success and personal gratification are. Social cohesion and conformity are guiding principles, and success is measured in worldly terms. It is questionable whether psychoanalytic theory contains any element of the Comic vision. Thus, theoreticians question the viability of the possibility of integration between CBT and psychodynamic modalities. It is only seen as possible for a therapist to take an eclectic approach. This is seen in cognitive-analytic therapy (Ryle and Kerr, 2002). To a limited extent, some analytic therapists will help the patient to pursue and attain the socially acceptable goals with which he may be struggling; however, the focus is usually upon internal, intrapsychic conflict rather than external obstacles. Admittedly, attachment theory, ego psychology (Kohut, 1971, 1977, 1984) and the intersubjective perspective (Stolorow et al., 1983, 1995) do accept that external difficulties such as one's attachment experience or traumatic events in childhood can lead to difficulty in surmounting negative circumstance. However, this appertains more to the Ironic and Tragic visions of reality because the focus is upon the way in which the protagonist personally and privately deals with problems and eventually comes to terms with his difficulties.

The Comic vision is far more hopeful than the Tragic or Ironic vision. The locus of responsibility is external – social difficulties are conceived as the problem rather than intrapsychic conflict. The locus of control is internal, however; it is the responsibility of the protagonist to remedy areas of difficulty that he encounters.

The power of agency is stressed, as are external, social problems, situations and circumstance. There is a preoccupation with structure; the individual must adapt to society, not vice versa. Happiness is attainable, although it needs to be striven for – so this vision is less positive in overall terms than the Romantic vision, because conflict and problems are acknowledged and seen as an integral part of life. The purpose in life is to live effectively in society; happiness is achieved by accommodating oneself to the social structure.

The Tragic Vision of Reality

The Tragic vision of reality is relatively negative; it is certainly the most pessimistic of the four visions of reality. It stresses the inescapable dangers in life, its terrors, dangers and absurdities. Schafer puts it eloquently when he says we need to recognise the elements of victory in defeat and of defeat in victory and of pain in pleasure and pleasure in pain (Shafer, 1976, p. 35).

We see, therefore, that even when having regard to the power of agency – the fact that the individual can make one choice rather than another – in the Tragic vision, the negative element of this is stressed: in making a certain choice, one is seen to renounce and forego other opportunities.

It is not difficult to recognise that we find that the Tragic vision shares the metatheoretical assumptions of the psychoanalytic theoretical orientation. It is also true that the prospective client who intuitively holds a Tragic vision of reality will tend to intuitively seek psychoanalytic psychotherapy or analysis if and when he decides upon pursuing a course of therapy. Here, 'cure' is not promised or even thought to be possible. The purpose of therapy is to come to terms with life's misfortunes and to appreciate how much better one feels when one has attained a fuller understanding of one's inner conflicts and the inevitability of difficulties encountered on the way through life. To paraphrase Freud's famous statement, "Psychoanalysis has done its job when neurotic misery is converted to everyday human unhappiness". There is no free lunch to be had! The view is summarised by the idea that only when experiencing the greatest adversity in life does one realise oneself most fully.

We shall see in a later chapter on Viktor Frankl that his development of logotherapy, of which he wrote the basics whilst interred as a Jew in Hitler's concentration camps, represents this vision of reality. It was only during his experience of the Holocaust, during which time he lost both of his parents, his wife and his brother to Hitler's tyranny, that Frankl came to appreciate the true value and purpose of suffering. This is not to deny his own personal trauma during the war. Indeed, he experienced a period of mental disturbance after the war as he struggled to come to terms with his dreadful experience and its attendant huge losses. But his message is – so truly Tragic in perspective – that there can be wisdom, resilience and an appreciation of the good in life borne out of suffering. There is no expectation of unmitigated joy; wisdom can only be achieved after one has experienced suffering and pain. It is also accepted that wisdom does not proceed *de rigueur* as a consequence of having suffered. One needs to make something positive from the negative experience.

Intrapsychic conflicts are stressed – there is a focus upon fixation, repression, regression, denial and the "repetition compulsion" so often spoken of by Freud (1914). One accepts that one can never come to rule the unconscious; that the best one can hope for is an understanding and diminution of the power of unconscious process: the sheer unconsciousness of the unconscious, as Nina Coltart called it. One understands that when a choice is taken, one appreciates and accepts that this involves sacrifice, ambivalence and remorse.

The past cannot be wiped out; if one's mother was a drug addict and treated one harshly and uncomprehendingly, one's childhood cannot be undone by any amount of therapy. However, it is possible to come to terms with one's experience; to learn to appreciate the circumstances that produced the addiction (in this case) and to grow psychically in consequence. Again, I stress, it is about coming to terms with reality and taking some learning from one's experiences.

The quest is often found to be resolved by the analytic process itself; frequently, the analysand engages in this with maximum determination. This is still to acknowledge that the difficulties of negative transference and resistance will take place; it is not envisaged as an easy journey. The analysand is seen as a Tragic protagonist or hero – though a different hero from that seen in the Romantic vision.

It has been said: "*Tout comprendre; c'est tout pardonner*". This is not seen as reality in analytic therapy. During my years as a therapist, I have had to stress to patients on many occasions that my role is not to offer absolution for any morally questionable behaviour; it is instead to help them to come to terms with and understand their past actions.

The loci of control and responsibility in the Tragic vision of reality are understood to be a mix of internal and external. None of us can change the past or the difficult times that we have suffered – in this way, the loci of responsibility and control are external. However, the future does not dictate that one is constrained to suffer forevermore; accommodation and acceptance are to be gained, and peace of mind earned. In this way, the loci are internal to the individual. There is a focus and insistence upon the past and how it skews the present, of the power of fate over agency. This vision of reality is, undoubtedly, the most pessimistic of the four visions.

The Ironic Vision of Reality

How, then, does the Ironic vision of reality differ from the Tragic vision? It also stresses the way that the past skews the present, and it is not anticipated that we negate or ignore the effect of past incidents upon us in today's world. However, it aims at detachment and the maintenance of a sense of perspective; it keeps life's negatives in proportion. It seeks to inform us and help us to appreciate how good can emanate from bad; that there is a purpose in life and we can create our own salvation. It seeks to turn over the metaphorical coin that we hold in the palm of our hand and to appreciate the flipside. Good can come from bad. 'Cure' is not promised, but indeed, we can grow and learn to feel a great deal better than we did before engaging in therapy or an introspective process.

As Schafer states, we learn that it is wise to be aware of the antithesis to any thesis so that we are capable of mitigating the effect of any thesis upon us (Shafer, 1976, p. 51). Everything is relative.

Schafer stresses that the Ironic view does not necessarily or inherently seek to withdraw or make a mockery of the life events that have befallen us. Life should be and is taken seriously (ibid, p. 51). The Ironic perspective attends equally to the external and to the internal, whereas the Tragic vision stresses only the internal world. The Ironic perspective plays down the emotional overcharge that is sometimes associated with the Tragic vision; it suppresses the tendency to grandiosity. Again, there is attention to the internal and external, to the inner and outer locus of control. This is a part of the process of keeping everything in perspective.

In analysis, it is felt that the Ironic vision leads to a deepening of the analytic process; it helps the analysand to keep the reality of the 'as if' in mind so he does not get subsumed by the erotic transference and extend it so that it becomes erotised.

The Ironic vision takes a measured view that falls between unmitigated pleasure and success and the contrary expectation of fatalistic acceptance of the inevitabilities of life.

Awareness of this will mean that one is not surprised to find that this is in line with those of us that take an eclectic or integrative theoretical orientation when in the consulting room. Admittedly, I have undergone psychoanalytic training, and my greater theoretical knowledge lies within the analytic paradigm, but in the practical atmosphere of the consulting room, I sometimes find a pragmatic approach to be most effective. It is true that I identify with the basic tenets of the psychoanalytic way of thinking – for me, the past does affect us in the present, it cannot be undone, and this is to be constantly borne in mind. Similarly, I believe in the dictum: "Analyse, analyse, analyse!" However, it seems to me that at times, there is room for differing theoretical modalities. It was with this in mind that I wrote a book (Fear, 2018) that uses cognitive and behavioural techniques as well as the intervention of transference interpretation and linking past to present in order to increase awareness. I use this approach when dealing with the treatment of panic disorder and phobia. I cannot accommodate the view that because I have undergone psychoanalytic training, when someone presents before me in a state of high tension, having suffered the disabling effects of panic disorder, I can refuse to help them when cognitive and behavioural skills can ease their distress in the short term. My experience of using these interventions pragmatically is that it greatly helps the individual to achieve a respite from the symptoms speedily. Psychoanalytic interventions can then be pursued alongside the cognitive and behavioural interventions and, indeed, can be attended to in the longer term in order to achieve enduring recovery for the individual.

However, the Ironic perspective is the enemy of the Romantic vision and differs greatly from the Comic. Whereas behaviour therapists (certainly those classically behaviourist) are more likely to accept the stated therapeutic aims of the client and to accept clients' complaints at face value (there is little room for introspection), the Ironic therapist takes nothing at face value. The therapist aims at detachment, at keeping things in perspective; and as I have reiterated before, she turns the coin over and focusses on the less obvious face of it. Nothing is taken for granted (Messer and Winokur, 1986, p. 117).

Discussion of Different World Views

You will hopefully now start to appreciate these four competing, very different world views. I hope, like me, that you find the philosophical debate – the epistemological challenge – of these visions of reality really fascinating. It is more than twenty-five years since my first introduction to them, but I remain fascinated by the dynamic between the visions. They vary in some ways and are at complete odds with one another; in other parts of their philosophy, they represent gradations. Thus, for example, the Tragic is the most pessimistic of the visions, followed by the Ironic. However, there is a distinctly optimistic stance within the Ironic vision, though it remains more negative in outlook than the Comic or Romantic vision. The Ironic stance does not countenance that perfection can be achieved. The Comic recognises and gives due credence to the negative but resolves that it is possible to circumnavigate the difficulties in life. The Romantic vision, in contrast, stresses the positive, the optimistic stance, looking at life from a rosy perspective, concentrating resolutely upon the opportunities rather than the constraints.

I have tried, in defining each of these visions of reality, to highlight a number of elements that they each approach from a differing standpoint. Namely, I have talked about each in terms of the loci of responsibility and control. The visions vary in the degree to which they circumscribe the loci as being external or internal to the individual. In this way, they ascribe differences in terms of the power of agency as opposed to the effects of structure.

I have attempted to tease out how each view stands on the optimism/pessimism continuum. I have tried to explain what they each consider to be the quest in life – the ultimate goal. I have also talked about the various elements that they each focus upon and where each vision stands in relation to the importance given to the past. In doing this, I have discussed the relative importance given to constraints versus opportunities.

I truly believe that you will need to be aware of the concept of differing world views and to appreciate the various nuances of these four visions in order to fully engage with the logic of my analysis of the research data in this book. However, it is to be remembered that it is not only in the analysis of stories here but that the world view adopted affects the narrative tone of every story that you read, although it is not often expressed consciously by the author.

Chapter 4

The Life of Patrick Casement

Introduction

By the time I entered the world of therapy, Patrick Casement's seminal first book, *On Learning From the Patient* (Casement, 1985), had become a best-seller. I firmly remember how influenced I was by his idea that it is to be expected that one makes mistakes and, indeed, that one can learn from mistakes by actually possessing the courage to process them with a supervisor or with the patient in the consulting room. This dictum gave me permission in those early days as a counsellor with Relate to try my very best in the consulting room but to feel neither deskilled nor disconsolate when I made a mistake. His words uphold what seems to me to be one of the most positive features of an individual's personality: that of humility. He put forward the view that we, as therapists, are no more 'all-knowing' or 'expert' than any of the patients with whom we work. This idea is so far from the 'all-knowing' refrain that Freud first taught in the new language of psychoanalysis, back in the late nineteenth and early twentieth centuries. And what a relief it was for a neophyte counsellor to be told this by Patrick Casement in those days of the early nineties!

Being 'Different From the Norm'?

Consequently, I have thoroughly enjoyed reading all of Patrick Casement's books, not least being the most recent one: *Growing Up? A Journey With Laughter* (Casement, 2015). This recent book of Casement's comprises an autobiography of his early years, covering in detail the years leading to his qualification as a psychoanalyst in 1971, with the addition of a moving tribute to the loss of his parents some years later. One of the themes that I rapidly discovered to appear in the data was evidence of the analyst being, in some way, 'different from the norm'. I found that I would suggest both Hanna (his elder daughter) and her father share an unusual, wry and whimsical sense of humour. This was seen in the way Hanna devised the notion of holding a grand family gathering on what would have been her grandfather's 100th birthday had he still been alive. As Patrick wryly observed, what sort of a family plans four funerals for two people and a party to commemorate them

DOI: 10.4324/9781003316503-5

years after they have departed this life? Patrick's whimsical sense of humour is one factor which shines forth and serves to amuse us in his autobiography; I have always been particularly moved by Patrick Casement's sense of humour, his rare talent to focus upon the funny (peculiar) side of life when the same event could equally be viewed from a tragic perspective. I believe that this facet in his character evidences two of my researched themes, the first providing an indication of his vision of reality (to which I will turn later). Secondly, Patrick's whimsy has enabled him to become a renowned psychoanalyst, for as Janet Malcolm (1997) so aptly named her book, it is *The Impossible Profession*! These same words were reiterated by Nina Coltart in *Slouching Towards Bethlehem* (Coltart, 1986, p. 2). Just think, as my own therapist declares: how many normal individuals would want to spend the majority of their lives delving into the inner worlds of the troubled people who present in their consulting rooms, day after day, year in and year out? Patrick's sense of humour is the first way that he definitely differs from the norm.

Yet another way in which I sense Patrick Casement's 'difference' can be seen is in the way he repeatedly provides us with instances of his disregard for authority. Again, I find this quality to occur several times in the lives of the individuals I have researched. For example, Patrick tells us, with unrestrained glee, about a piano teacher (a Miss Duggie) whose wrist he broke in one of his skirmishes with authority whilst at prep school (Casement, 2015, p. 31). In another instance, he tells us drolly how he decided one year, as a boy, to give his senior relatives each a fistful of elastic bands as his Christmas present to them (Casement, 2015, p. 59)!

Patrick Casement's Vision of Reality

I would now like to move on to the way that Patrick's whimsical sense of humour evidences a particularly clear world view. Namely, I am highlighting the manner in which Patrick magically finds humour and relief in what could so equally be viewed as Tragic. There are four world views that could possibly appear in my analysis of the texts: Tragic, Ironic, Romantic and Comic. The reader will see that I have noted that most talented psychoanalytic therapists are wont to hold either a Tragic or an Ironic vision of reality. Patrick's capacity to seek and derive amusement from dark material evidences his holding an Ironic world view. Essentially, this signifies an individual who is motivated to turn the coin over and to look at the other side. One effectively says (to mix my metaphors!), "I have been dealt this amazingly poor hand of cards, but let me see, how can I utilise them so as to make a winning hand of cards?" In this way, the individual with an Ironic vision of reality reverses the coin and calls forth something positive from his ill luck. Surely this is the essence of how one can surmount the idea that fate controls all, and by contrast, gives the upper hand to the spirit of free will. We see here the epistemological argument of determinism versus free will. The Ironic vision holds the belief that life is what you make of it with the cards you have been dealt – as opposed to living your life with blinkers on, hoping against hope that nothing bad will ever befall you (as in the Romantic world view). By employing an Ironic vision of reality, one determines, instead, to make the best of what actually occurs in one's life.

Patrick's Quest in Life

I can find plenty of evidence in Patrick Casement's autobiography that provides us with his essentially optimistic stance on life. He tells us how he spent a year in Sheffield after he had graduated from Cambridge. He emerged from Cambridge University with a 2:1, which he was told would have been a First but for his archaeology paper. In fact, he had initially chosen to read for a degree in theology and anthropology, as he admits he had no idea what he would like to study when he accepted a place at Cambridge University. With a typical disdain for convention, he chose anthropology because whilst he did not know what it entailed, someone whimsically had informed him that it entailed the study of man embracing women! He thought that the idea of this was extremely appealing (Casement, 2015, p. 145)! Emerging from one of the two most prestigious universities in England, after senior schooling at the similarly renowned Winchester College, many boys went on to commence illustrious careers. However, in Patrick's case, it seems his decision regarding a career was overshadowed by two concerns. Firstly, he wanted at all costs to avoid being propelled into a career in the Royal Navy. Every male on his father's side of the family from grandfather (as a commander) onwards had enjoyed formidable careers in the Royal Navy, including his elder brother, Michael, who followed in their father's footsteps. Contrarily, Patrick was fiercely determined not to succumb to this family tradition. Symbolically, I think that this is the reason that Patrick chose for the cover of his autobiography a photograph depicting he and his brother as children, dressed in sailor suits, attempting a salute. It is with wry humour that one becomes aware of how Patrick always veers from the norm, evidenced by the fact that the photograph depicts him making a crooked salute (not really liking being photographed in this manner), standing slightly at an angle to the camera (unlike his elder brother, who stands directly facing the camera, making a serious salute).

The second preoccupation regarding career seems to have been either a conscious or semi-conscious determination to find something meaningful to do with his life. In other words, he possessed an urge to search for and to answer a quest: the wish to pursue a career that would become a passion. Maybe it was for this reason that Patrick seriously considered working towards ordination as a priest and devoting his life to God, and he did indeed spend some significant period of time deciding if this career would answer his wish to follow a quest. The holding of a quest is another of the themes/categories that I found in my analysis of the texts. I believe that the fact that he was wont to follow a quest explains the reason he tried quite a number of career choices before he found psychoanalysis. If one holds a quest, it takes the shape of the individual consistently being engaged in an existential search to find true meaning in life. I think that Patrick, like others in my research, tended to be asking of himself: "What makes people/me tick?" "What is the inner meaning of life?" "How is one to come to terms with suffering?"

It seems to me that Patrick's interest in theology and the thought of joining the Church, early in life, was a function of a number of factors. Firstly, undeniably, the Church was at the centre of his early years, amongst those institutions which remained unchanged throughout his childhood. The constancy of the Church helped him to create a sense of security in a world in which his parents lived a peripatetic Navy lifestyle. His parents repeatedly moved location not only to different regions in Britain but throughout the world. He speaks in his autobiography with tenderness about the church at Terwick – the little church just beyond the village where his parents owned the Old Rectory. He remembers with fondness the times he spent singing in church choirs – at Winchester College and even at Winchester Cathedral during one summer vacation. He talks with affection of the organ and some of its players with whom he was familiar. He movingly states that music saved his sanity at Winchester (Casement, 2015, p. 95). So I surmise that the Church and its teachings provided him with a sense of security through its constant presence during his early years. Religion has helped, I would suggest, to answer his quest in life.

Following upon his graduation and consequent decision that he might like to enter the Church, he spent a year in Sheffield, deciding whether to become a probation officer. I would surmise from his description that it was a tough year, for the first six months were spent working as a brickie's mate (Casement, 2015, pp. 166–167, and photograph on p. 164), and during this time, he carried out a variety of tasks that required real physical stamina. Again, it is interesting to note that he felt that it was important to gain acceptance by a wide range of individuals from social classes quite different from his own. He is rightly proud that he was quickly accepted "as one of the lads", known as Pat, despite the fact that his work-mates teased him about his 'posh' voice. Again, I think that it is a function of his Ironic vision of reality that enables him to take on board whatever circumstances dictated. He is able to mould himself, to be accepted, whether that is in spending time with a retired prostitute, a single mother with a bunch of children from different fathers, or with the queen of England (described in Casement, 2015, pp. 236–237). And despite the fact that he is able to mould himself, it is never at the expense of losing his inimitable sense of identity.

Attachment Difficulties and Evidence of Trauma in Early Years

I believe that it is a function of Patrick's unique sense of identity and 'difference' that led to him being renowned as a difficult child within the home and at prep school (Maidwell, near Nottingham). He recalls that he and brother Michael were looked after by a rapid succession of nannies. Evidently, many nannies quickly vacated the post as a consequence of his being envisaged as "a difficult child" (Casement, 2006, p. 23). One nanny (Tucky) stayed for years, and it is clear he was attached to her despite the evident thrill he took in making her red-faced with fury and frustration (Casement, 2015, p. 13.) His mother, aware that despite her son's difficult nature, he was also emotionally sensitive, tried to ease his guilt by telling him that Tucky had eventually left the family because she did not want to look after his two younger sisters, who were still babies. When he heard that she was leaving, he remembers crying himself to sleep for several weeks because he believed he had been so naughty that Tucky could no longer suffer his behaviour (Casement, 2006, p. 26). In fact, when he met the infamous Tucky in adulthood, she told him that she had left simply because he was so impossible (Casement, 2006, pp. 25–26)! However, he adds wryly – and characteristically – he is not sure whether she was still teasing him in her old age!

Undeniably, by his own admittance, he was difficult to discipline. He quotes how his Maidwell headmaster called him to his study to inform him in no uncertain terms that all the staff had given up on him because he was so impossible. However, the headmaster proposed to try something that no-one else had attempted: he had decided to give Patrick ('Casement Two') a responsible role by making him a school prefect. It seems this device worked very well, but Patrick is unsure whether he personally relished the outcome – he felt that he forwent his rebellious streak for a time, a pity because he considers this an essential part of his character. It occurs to me that he derived a distinctive part of his sense of identity from his reputation as 'difficult'. Once again, this self-perception provides us with more evidence that he visualises himself as 'different from the norm'. He tells us with glee how on one occasion he 'misunderstood' the headmaster's command of "Don't hurry!" as a literal rather than satirical statement whilst he was being asked to translate some Latin text!

I have spoken earlier about the fact that his parents moved house innumerable times during his formative years. In consequence, he informs us that he perceived his departure to boarding school at age eight as one of the best decisions that his parents ever made. It is not unusual for past pupils of boarding school to resent the fact that they were shunted off from home at a tender age. Once again, Patrick, with his inimitable Ironic vision of reality, turns this potential negative into a positive. Never once bemoaning the loss of intimate contact at home, Patrick perceives that the two schools he attended provided him with a sense of security that was lacking due to his parents' nomadic lifestyle. I interpret this fact in two ways. Firstly, it provides us with a paradigm for his Ironic stance on life.

Secondly, this assertion also provides us with a clear indication that Patrick probably suffered from an insecure attachment schema, a sub-optimal level of attachment, yet he was able to find and hold onto key relationships. Again, this is one of the themes/categories that I have analysed in reading about the lives of these therapists. Indeed, it points to the individuals being wounded in some way. In *Learning From Life: Becoming a Psychoanalyst* (Casement, 2006, p. 29), Patrick tells us that he was "showing an attachment to places rather than people. I had too often experienced people as unreliable. They kept on leaving". For example, he clearly remembers his father as "mostly absent" (ibid, p. 25). These two statements point to the way I suspect Patrick suffered as a result of an extended period of trauma in his early life. To put this finding in perspective, it is not withstanding that many of us suffer from sub-optimal attachment experiences (34%, according to Van-Ijzendoorn and Kroonenberg, 1988) without going on in life to become wounded healers. I suspect that one needs to have the full range of qualities in order to follow one's quest by becoming a therapist.

Nevertheless, it is my opinion that those individuals who decide, either by making a conscious decision or by serendipity, to take a path which leads them to become therapists glean a sense of hitherto unfulfilled satisfaction from the sense of intimacy that they derive from their clinical work. I believe that they are partially motivated to make this choice of career as a result of intimacy difficulties in their attachment history. Such individuals have known either one of two experiences, which I will elucidate in what follows. First (and less commonly), they may have suffered an experience of 'merging' with a parental figure during their formative years. Such individuals deeply miss this sense of being connected in such an intense way that when it is lost, they unconsciously seek to replicate it in the career of their choice; to gain, once again, that hard-to-replicate 'at one' feeling with another individual they deem to be a soulmate. A second and more common scenario involves a situation in which the individual finds that he consciously or unconsciously yearns for a sense of 'connection' – an emotional closeness which he has always found lacking in his life and which, when found, would add to the meaning to life. I think Patrick Casement lacked this sense of connection because of his parents' constant change of locations and their physical absence during his years at boarding school. However, I think he deeply yearned to achieve this connection. From what little he tells us about his marriage to Margaret, I think he found this sense of connection once he met her whilst he was at the Family Welfare Association (FWA). He evidences his sensitivity and ability to appreciate fine feelings and to feel deeply when he tells us, with no apology, that Hanna was the most beautiful baby ever (Casement, 2015, p. 224). But maybe the fact that this intimacy was lacking in his formative years has given him a 'hunger' that was not to be satiated by his personal relationships alone in his early adulthood. I strongly contend that he found his way, through a maze of assorted experiences (brickie's mate, supply teacher, probation officer, family welfare officer, psychoanalytic psychotherapist) into the world of psychoanalysis in order to unconsciously – maybe consciously – satisfy this hunger.

Imagine how it must have been for a teenager to be told by his mother that it was not worth the travel expenses (Casement, 2015, p. 94) for him to join the family for the summer vacation! In consequence, he spent school holidays (or parts of them) with the matron or with his singing teacher (Mrs. Blake) or with his grandmother. It moves me a great deal to think of the feeling of abandonment that he may have suffered as a result of what may have been an insensitive, albeit practical, pecuniary measure. No wonder that being chosen to sing in Winchester Cathedral during one of the holidays meant so much to him!

Whilst Patrick Casement did not – fortunately – suffer any one-off identifiable traumatic incident in his childhood, I believe he was traumatised by the effects of his father's nomadic lifestyle in the Navy. A period of traumatisation is yet another category/theme that my research has uncovered. The outcome of such a trauma to Patrick, I suggest, led to the resulting hunger for connection and a quest to find a solution to this feeling.

I find it fascinating that Patrick recounts how during his adult years, he took to chatting to his mother in her bedroom just before she retired to bed. This occurred so frequently that his mother devised a way of undressing whilst talking to him without displaying her nakedness – by undressing beneath the cover of her night-gown. I believe he treasures this memory because he is not only wryly amused by the transparency of her nightgown – thus negating the point of her shenanigans – but also because it represented times when he felt emotionally close to her. In a similar manner, he talks with evident fondness about an occasion when the whole family managed to be together in Malta (Casement, 2015, p. 131) during his period of National Service. At another time at prep school, he warmly recalls that the Maidwell Headmaster especially took the care to bring him a book on cosmology and astronomy, having learned that Patrick had been looking at the stars from the dormitory window. His interest in cosmology has never waned (Casement, 2015, p. 25). Similarly, Patrick revered a music master at Winchester, Henry Havergal (Casement, 2015, p. 99), who served the role of mentor to him for a time. Ah, the effect of having been treated as special!

Experience of Mental Disturbance?

Lastly, I cannot bring to an end an analysis of Patrick Casement's life story, gravitating towards his career as a therapist, without commenting upon his time spent in mental hospital, ostensibly suffering from a nervous breakdown (Casement, 2006, pp. 36–44). Patrick remembers this time as an example of how *not* to be treated in a mental hospital. I am sure that the fact that he only received fifteen minutes of personal contact with a doctor throughout his stay represents dreadful neglect (as was typical in psychiatric wards during that era), but maybe the respite he experienced from the pressures of day-to-day living did prove beneficial. I am aware that Doctor Stewart Prince, a Home Office consultant and Jungian analyst, preferred to believe in Patrick's version of what happened in hospital, but I think that whilst the experience was no doubt very painful, plus it was distressing to find that it put his training as a social worker at Barnet House in jeopardy, I believe Patrick may have gained from the experience in a number of ways. First, it provided him with insight into how not to treat individuals undergoing emotional and mental crises in their lives, for it provided evidence of the value and necessity of therapeutic 'holding' (something sadly absent from his own experience). Secondly, he was able to learn – painfully, no doubt – firsthand how the cumulative effect of difficult events (especially when they resonate with one's own personal vulnerabilities) can overwhelm any individual temporarily and bring normal living to a halt for a period of time. Looking at the experience from an Ironic perspective – most experiences, however painful and difficult to survive – can be transformative in that we can certainly grow as a result of our suffering. It tends to be true that it is after such painful times rather than after periods of unadulterated happiness that we grow.

Conclusion

I have certainly found Patrick Casement's two autobiographical books endearing and fascinating. I imagine that many of us would choose to be in analysis with this man. That is always a strong test for those of us who are therapists to decide if we would choose to be in therapy with a particular person. However, my analysis of his life story provides supporting evidence that those therapists who develop a sense of vocation during their careers do possess a number of the characteristics of 'wounded healers'. However, this is not to say that individuals enter the therapy world in order to heal themselves; rather that their acquired sensitivity to 'wound-edness' means that they are drawn to help others who are suffering in a way with which they are familiar. In conclusion, I draw attention to the way in which early life experiences affect that sense of personal 'woundedness'. Such individuals suffer their own less-than-optimal attachment schema and consequently crave the emotional sense of connection that one gains by being part of the therapy dyad. Why else is it that some of us are so keen to listen to the woes and anguish of others for hours at a time each day? It would be nice to say that it is sheer altruism, but I think we must receive a personal payoff to persist in this endeavour.

Patrick, like so many other therapists, has endured his own personal brush with mental illness, and this constitutes another of the themes that I deduced from my research. In my opinion, this can only serve to increase our capacity for empathic understanding. I believe that Patrick, too, having sailed in choppy seas through difficult periods of loneliness in two boarding schools and a turbulent time in National Service, has wondered about the meaning of life. Lastly but perhaps most importantly, I want to comment upon Patrick Casement's *weltanschauung*: his Ironic world view. When I ponder the philosophy of his two first books, *On Learning From the Patient* (1985) and *Further Learning From the Patient* (1990), is he not providing us in these books with a practical application of an Ironic vision of reality? Effectively, he is saying: "Take a mistake that you have made; admit it to yourself and talk it through with others; above all, take some learning from it". I find his way of writing fascinating and endearing.

Chapter 5

The Life of Neville Symington

Introduction

Neville Symington was born in 1937, the third child of his parents. His family were of English nationality and were fierce supporters of the Roman Catholic Church, unlike most of the English contingent in Oporto, where he was raised. However, the family had a foot in the camp of the indigenous population, as Neville's paternal grandmother was half Portuguese. His mother was born in Australia but had actually first come to Oporto to visit a friend, Audrey, and whilst there, she met her husband to be. The couple married a year later in London. Within a few years, Neville's mother gave birth first to James and then to Jill. Neville believes that his sister was the love of his mother's life, because she preferred females to males. Mother maintained a very close relationship with her daughter, to whom she 'clung'. Her elder son, James, made his father his closest ally. So who should Neville make his primary attachment object?

Neville Symington's Trauma in Early Life: Attachment History

Neville felt that his mother positively had not wanted a third child and certainly would have preferred this child to be female. He believes that he unconsciously introjected this hope, so in unconscious response, he became a 'female boy' in order to try to satisfy his mother's desires. He understood that the fact that she tended to cling to him (too) like a limpet was in response to a deep sense of emptiness that she experienced throughout her life. This clinginess was paradoxically not experienced as a secure attachment, for it is based on neediness of the object. Neville sensed that his mother's behaviour may have resulted from the emptiness she felt in her emotionally sterile marriage.

When Neville was three years old, he was separated from his beloved father when he and his siblings were evacuated to Canada with their mother for three years to escape the ravages of the Second World War. He poignantly remembers how his father placed in his hands a string bag of farm animals, hoping to lessen the pain of separation. It might have been better had his father offered him some words

DOI: 10.4324/9781003316503-6

of comfort and understanding. I guess these farm animals may have been images of poignant longing. He also remembers particularly the pain of being parted from his nanny, Joan Smith, and how he "howled" as the train drew out of the platform. Both nanny and father were central to what sense of security he had managed to achieve, so the move to Canada was experienced as catastrophic. He remembers trying, from age three, to make up for his father's disappointment in life. I think perhaps Neville tried resolutely to hold onto a perception that he was an integral part of a large, loving family. Indeed, his nuclear family enjoyed the geographical proximity of their extended family network, but in fact, it seems questionable whether they were a loving family in reality, as will be explained later in the chapter. At other times in his autobiography, Neville describes himself as being totally engulfed by a feeling of pessimism that fed his inner state of "damned impoverishment" (Symington, 2016, p. 11). This does not seem to resonate with the concept that he was held securely within a tight-knit family. Admittedly, he fondly remembers his participation in the cricket matches where it was, in effect, the enormous clan of the extended Symington family against the other side (ibid, p. 15). This was a consequence of being part of an extended family consisting of his father's three siblings and nine first cousins. Perhaps it more accurately explains that his father stubbornly refused to relinquish his primary attachment to his family of origin. Maybe this is the reason it proved impossible for him to create an emotionally satisfying primary relationship with his wife, who did not belong to this group.

Indeed, Neville's father was welded to his extended family structure in Oporto, where he and his brothers all worked within the port trade. Neville's father was very close to his twin brother, John, and his wife, Aileen. The twin brothers had been sent, as per the norm in upper-middle-class families, to be educated at public boarding school – at The Oratory in Birmingham. Whilst they were pupils there at the tender age of twelve, two unknown ladies arrived at the school one day and took the children aside to inform them that their mother had died.

It seems that Neville's father never recovered from this grief; this loss was echoed for him in his disappointment with his marriage. It is possible that the emotional gulf that existed between Neville's parents was also partially due to his father's pious, self-righteous devotion to the Roman Catholic Church and all of its demands – demands that Neville's mother experienced as alienating.

It appears that Neville's supposition that his mother preferred women may well have been accurate, because in mid-life, when his mother felt free to satisfy her own desires, she embarked upon a public affair with a woman called Clay. Neville wonders whether, in fact, this was his mother's first lesbian relationship – for there existed some evidence that she had enjoyed an infatuation with another young woman, Jane Webster, whilst still living as a young woman in Australia. In addition, during her early years of mothering, Neville's mother spent a lot of time with a close friend, Clare Waters, with whom Neville feels she may also have had a sexual relationship.

It is partially as a result of Neville's mother's predilection for the female gender that Neville surmised that his mother would have liked him to be a girl. He feels that his mother rejected him whilst he was in the womb, leaving him with a prenatal experience of insecurity. In terms of attachment schema, it seems that Neville grew up feeling very insecure, neither securely attached to his mother nor contained by his father. His father's piety and obsession with the Catholic faith, combined with his view of God as a sadistic God of the Old Testament who demanded that He be replenished by His followers because He had suffered the loss of His only son at the Crucifixion, left Neville with a deeply held belief system which perpetuated for quite a number of years of his adult life. He realised later in life that he wanted to believe in a giving, generous God who loved his servants upon earth and was compassionate and loving. He was deeply affected, as already mentioned, by his separation from his father when his mother took the children to Canada, and in fact he talks of this parting bearing visible traces of the earlier rejection that had occurred in the womb (ibid, p. 111).

Neville's memory of early childhood was dominated by a certain Easter Sunday when he was three years of age. His father commanded that all the family accompany him to church, but Neville knew he had actually eaten something earlier in the morning and that it was a mortal sin to eat before taking Communion. Nevertheless, Neville accompanied the family to church, and as a result of this, he was then plagued for years by the notion that he was doomed to damnation, because he had committed (what he understood as) two mortal sins – the first by taking Communion and the second by failing to confess to the priest at the earliest opportunity.

He remembers making this momentous decision to take communion, and thus face damnation, simply as a result of trying at all costs to avoid disappointing his father any further. Thus, it would seem, by the age of three, he had introjected his father's deep sense of disappointment and 'woundedness'. Neville felt that this disappointment grew, as his father was also deeply disappointed with the emotional sterility of his marriage, a feeling that most likely grew in intensity when his wife proceeded to engage in a rather public lesbian affair.

Neville loved spending time with his father, to whom he longed to feel close. However, he also felt irresistibly drawn by his mother's clingy behaviour and the way he describes what the researcher interprets as a feeling of 'merging' with her. He described how this 'merged state' was aroused as a consequence of his mother's mesmerising stare. It is this historical experience of 'merging' that I believe has since forced him to search, unconsciously, for experiences in life which 'echo' this feeling of deep connection. It is true that one can gain this at times in one's life as a psychotherapist or psychoanalyst. The author would suggest that some of us may choose this career as a way of hoping to re-experience those occasions of deep intimacy in the therapeutic setting. Contrarily, however, Neville also felt at a distance from his mother; perhaps this began because his first memories were of Mother sitting with her left leg resting on a stool, supporting her tubercular knee, in a plaster cast. He tells us that he experienced an abiding feeling that he could never get close enough to her. Could this be what Andre Green (Green, 1983) refers to as "the dead mother syndrome"? Green talks at length about the way that a mother who is emotionally unavailable to her baby is effectively 'dead' in the child's mind, because she cannot be reached even though she is physically present.

Despite conflicted feelings about his attachment to Mother, Neville describes a strong sense that he and his mother were 'partners' and that she shared this sensation, too. Maybe this is partly as a result of her clingy behaviour and the fact that her love was mixed with neediness. In such cases, it is not possible for the baby to learn containment from Mother, who needs to be able to hold and combine all the paranoid-schizoid bits of her child (as Melanie Klein believed) before she hands them back to the child. Mother needs to effectively process the churned-up, shattered bits of the baby's psyche – the bits he is not able to hold for himself – and return them to him in a manageable form. It seems that Neville's mother was not able to do this, perhaps because of her visceral sense of emptiness.

Perhaps in consequence of the sense of 'partnership' which Neville felt at times, he may not have been able to resolve the Oedipus complex at the genital stage of psychosexual development. In my book on the subject of the Oedipus complex, I present a case study of 'Frank' (Fear, 2016, pp. 61–75), who similarly found that he had regarded his mother as his partner; interestingly, this again was partly as a consequence of her intense hypnotic stare. This leads me in turn to the parallel with William Shakespeare's character Hamlet. You may remember that Hamlet could not abide his mother's remarriage to his uncle after the death of his father. Despite his unresolved oedipal strivings, he had been able to stomach his mother's marriage to his biological father, but he could not bear her to choose another partner other than himself. In Act IV, Scene iii, we are provided with evidence of his fury and disdain for her as he tries to impel her to refuse her new husband access to the marriage bed. In a fit of pure rage, he mistakenly believes his uncle is hiding behind the wall hangings and plunges a dagger into the man's belly. He finds that he has mistakenly killed Ophelia's father. He and Ophelia had been lovers prior to his father's death. As a consequence of the loss of her father and Hamlet's rejection of her, Ophelia takes her own life – depicted famously in Millais's Pre-Raphaelite painting of Ophelia's body sailing down the river, drowned (see book cover of Fear, 2016).

One wonders whether Neville's response to his mother taking a lover echoes Hamlet's behaviour – the huge difficulty in coming to terms with the idea that his mother could love someone other than his father and, indeed, a woman too. He describes the years that followed his learning of her affair as years of madness (Symington, 2016, p. 113). He says that it seemed to be so contrary to the whole set of values within which he had been raised. Having heard about his mother's lesbian relationship, he quickly absented himself from Clay's apartment (where he had been staying) and, unconsciously motivated, he entered college in order to train as a priest. Perhaps he felt by this act he would ally himself to his pious father whilst at the same time punishing his mother who deeply disliked her husband's church.

A Conscious Awareness of a Quest in Life

It seems Neville did enjoy much of his studies and remained determined to be ordained but nevertheless could not be reconciled to the nature of the Catholic God to whom he was proposing to devote his life. In fact, he actually was ordained and went on to participate as a priest in the East End of London for three and a half years. He describes himself as hating some aspects of the job. He particularly disliked living alongside Tony Beagle, the parish priest. This man stood for all the mediocrity and pious self-righteousness that Neville had so detested in his father. As he correctly summarises, it is the death to one's heart if you don't give yourself succour (ibid, p. 59) and speak out about what you believe. The willingness of one to speak out, no matter the effect, was very important to Neville, and he talks about the self-respect he gained in life as a consequence of daring to speak out and stand up for beliefs that truly matter to him. This willingness to make sure that he is heard, despite the fact that it may lead to rejection and animosity, is felt by Neville to be one of the personality traits of which he is most proud.

He speaks about the idea of pursuing a 'quest' in life: the essence, in his opinion, is to discover one's true self. He sagely remarked that a psychotherapist who has undergone a rigorous eight-year training yet does not know his true self will never make a successful psychotherapist. It is that ability to offer an interpretation to a patient, an interpretation which comes from the true self and is received as a meeting of souls, which brings with it the most profound healing (ibid, p. 21–22).

'Woundedness'

Shortly after ordination and having said his first Mass in London with both of his parents' present, he waved goodbye to his father (who was taking a flight back to Oporto) whilst he set out with his mother on a five-day road trip overland to Portugal. He remembered this vividly not least because he found to his dismay that he had nothing to say to her on the journey. He perceived their relationship to now be empty. This may be a function of the continuing anger he felt towards his mother for her betrayal.

After three and a half years as a priest, Neville realised that his God was not the God that was worshipped in the Roman Catholic Church, and in consequence, he was given a sabbatical to decide what course of action he proposed to take. He spoke of acting with a death wish at this time. He says in the autobiography that he believed that if one were to purposefully kill someone else, one is bad, whereas to kill oneself means that one is mad (Symington, 2016, p. 43). It is clear Neville acted in a 'mad' fashion for the next few years. He managed to avoid incarceration in a mental hospital or convalescent home but in fact wondered if that might have been a better option. After six months, he took the decision to leave the Church permanently. To leave the Church after ordination was considered a mortal sin. He felt in exile because his father communicated to him that it would be embarrassing for him to come home to Portugal. He received a very condemnatory letter from his Uncle John, who subsequently refused to communicate with him again, not even sending him a greeting card at Christmas. Neville effectively felt that he been cast out from his dearly beloved extended-family structure. It needs to be said, however, that both his parents wrote letters of support and love. He adds that his father said that nothing he could do would alter his love for Neville. Neville says that he needed to know this, perhaps because he had never known what it was to be securely attached.

He felt that his mother, too, showed unqualified love. When she was close to death some years later, he said remorsefully that he was sorry to have caused her so much pain. He felt that she showed great forgiveness and love by her reply that she could not remember a time when he had hurt her.

Neville Symington's life story evidences an insecure ambivalent attachment schema, to use the typology of attachment styles that was developed by Mary Ainsworth, the co-founder (with John Bowlby) of attachment theory. The evidence that I have gathered seems to indicate that it is essentially this lack of secure attachment that is central to the sense of 'woundedness' that so many therapists endure. It is accurate to say that we as therapists are not alone in suffering from insecure attachment. In fact, a third of the population in Western Europe suffer from less-than-optimal attachment styles (34%, according to Van Ijzendoorn and Sagi-Schwartz, 2008). The seminal point is that we do not only suffer from insecure attachment, which is accompanied by a sense of 'woundedness'. In addition, for other reasons (perhaps as a result of genetic endowment, perhaps as a result of early trauma), some of us have become sensitised to the wounds of others and have an unconscious urge to provide some salve to those wounds. Having analysed the texts using grounded theory, I believe that individuals who have missed out on this feeling of security in childhood yearn to achieve this sense of emotional connectedness in order to repair the deprivation they suffered in early years.

Neville Symington clearly felt insecurely attached, finding it difficult to feel close to his parents. In early childhood, he remembers spending hours in the company of the two maids, Carmen and Maria. He says that he achieved a sense of connection with them that he found difficult to match in his relationship with either parent. Perhaps, as he describes himself as not a typical boy who would fit in with a class of other boys, he is right to say that the English public school system was disastrous for individuals like himself (Symington, 2016, p. 81). He has evidently found it easier to make close relationships with men rather than with women, and it is clear he has achieved this sense of intimacy with a number of people he mentions in his autobiography. However, it is my contention that because he did experience that sense of 'merging' with his mother as a result of her mesmerising powers, he yearned to re-experience this sense of soul meeting soul again. This, I believe, is one of the central reasons that some individuals are drawn to a career as a therapist.

'Different From the Norm'?

The words that repeatedly come to mind regarding the wounds of Neville Symington were, in fact, used by his analyst, John Klauber, on a number of occasions. Neville brings these words to mind in his autobiography a number of times: Klauber's repeating sentiment was that he had suffered a massive disappointment and was, in fact, very ill. Neville was relieved to have this reality acknowledged.

Neville's life was marked by a series of disappointments. Firstly, Neville suffered a pre-natal sense of rejection because he perceived that his mother did not want him as a foetus. Additionally, Neville was sure that she would have preferred to have given birth to a girl. It may well be, then, that Neville, when he was born, represented a massive disappointment to her. It is perhaps a consequence of this unconscious sense of not being wanted or welcomed into the family that Neville was fairly sickly as a child. He developed asthma, bronchial problems, hay fever and eczema. At Ampleforth College, which he refers to amusingly but painfully as "Yorkshire's concentration camp" (Symington, 2016, p. 31), Neville became known by the derogatory nickname of Scaley – a reflection of the reddening, peeling, broken and blotchy skin he suffered as a result of severe eczema. This must have been most uncomfortable for a sensitive lad who clearly had no control whatsoever over the state of his skin (though it may have been a psychosomatic manifestation of his stressed-out state), and it was just one way in which he felt bullied by some of his schoolmates. As he says in his autobiography on a number of occasions, English boarding schools are no place for any child who is out of the ordinary or handicapped in some way. Public boarding schools are renowned for their ability to create men and women who develop an emotional resilience that enables them to deal with the emotional crises in their lives. They generally are regarded as having an outer barrier of 'phlegm', but as a side effect, they also tend to lack the capacity to be in touch with their feelings. This certainly does not apply to Neville Symington; no doubt he did not fit the image of 'successful' boys at boarding school.

It also seems to be true that the young Neville introjected his father's deep, ingrained sense of disappointment in life. Of course, in later years, his father's disappointment in his emotionally sterile marriage may have grown more pronounced as he suffered the ignominy of society's knowledge of his wife's long-term lesbian affair. One of the various reasons that Neville's mother engaged in an affair may have been that she believed that the love of her husband's life was actually Aileen (his sister-in-law), who nevertheless had chosen to marry his twin brother, John.

As a consequence, Neville grew up amid the enduring feeling that it was his responsibility to ameliorate his father's abiding sense of disappointment in life. This is, indeed, a huge burden for a young child to carry and goes quite some way towards reducing one's sense of carefree childhood. One tends to develop the role of 'enabler': to find a role in life in which one is committed to helping others to provide succour for their wounds. It seems that Neville and other 'subjects' of the research have all ingested an acute awareness of other's wounds. This has served them well in the following of their vocation as therapists. Indeed, it is this characteristic that I feel makes Neville 'different from the norm'.

Experience of Mental Disturbance

Neville Symington, by his own admission, suffered a long period of mental disturbance after he learnt of his mother's affair. First, he entered the Church but gradually grew to realise that the God of the Roman Catholic Church was not 'his God'. Three and a half years after ordination, he left the Church. He wonders if it would have been wiser at this time to have entered some mental hospital or convalescent home.

Instead, left to cope in the everyday world, he made another faulty and foolhardy decision; he met and married – in haste – a lady called Josephine who lived in Cromer. She was a widow with two children, whose husband Paul had quite recently taken his own life. Neville's marriage to Josephine was a disaster, as she constantly berated him for not being able to match up to her first husband. After fourteen long months, Neville left Josephine, shortly after she attempted to take her own life. The divorce proceedings and the settlement cost him all that he had inherited from his grandfather. A costly experiment in terms of finance and emotional distress! It seems that his decision to marry was a function of his abiding sense of aloneness which he was unconsciously – or maybe consciously – seeking to assuage. Or could it have been a part of a death wish?

During this period, he also applied to the Institute of Psychoanalysis to train as an analyst. It seems that the two assessors failed to recognise the level of his disturbance at that time! He was offered a place on the training after some initial disagreement as to whether he should first complete his degree in psychology at Brunel. This meant that he changed therapists to start work with his training analyst, John Klauber. This proved to be a very fortuitous move, for Klauber recognised the depths of his despair and his disturbance. He started his training analysis in April 1970, and he tells us that it became the focal point of his life for seven years (until he qualified as an associate member in 1977). These years following his departure from the Catholic Church were regarded by Neville as the worst in his life. They represented a protracted period of time in which he was suffering a profound level of mental disturbance. However, it seems that one's time of suffering in fact enables one to become a successful therapist with a strong sense of vocation. I wonder whether it is possible for one to accompany one's patients unless one has suffered substantially oneself. I doubt it.

Gradually, Neville found that as he was taken into confidence by a patient in the consulting room, the person gave him more than he felt he gave them. Does this statement not succeed in precisely summing up the possible motivation of the therapist who becomes a wounded healer?

Inch by inch, Neville pulled himself out of his mental crisis. He began analysis; he began his training as an analyst; he finished his degree in psychology at Brunel;

he found employment at Grendon prison in Buckinghamshire (which was the only therapeutic community as part of the prison system in England). Neville attributes a lot of his recovery to the healing powers of John Klauber. Whilst Neville does not feel that he actually loved his analyst, he deeply appreciated his generosity of spirit and his honesty in spite of the good-humoured distance in which Klauber chose to work.

In 1980, Neville was made a full professional member of the Institute of Psychoanalysis, and during this process of training as an analyst, he met (in 1973) Joan Cornwall (also a trainee) and married her a year later in 1974. He remained married to her for the rest of his life, and they had two sons. It does not seem too difficult to suggest that the healing power of analysis enabled him to at last achieved a capacity to enjoy a truly intimate personal relationship. Maybe the experience of a good, reliable and emotionally available object during his relationship with his analyst meant that he really did incorporate and internalise this object after his time in analysis had passed (Symington, 1996, p. 101).

Neville Symington's World View

It seems to me that Neville Symington has suffered far more trauma in his early years of both childhood and adulthood than many of us. Clearly, he suffered from a prolonged experience of insecure attachment and was traumatised by a sense that his mother did not welcome him into her life, the effect of his mother's affair upon him, by his life at boarding school and the overarching experience of a disappointed father who was obsessed with a punishing God. Further trauma ensued from his hasty first marriage. However, he seems to me to have coped with all these adversities in life and nevertheless has not allowed these events to detract from his capacity to make an incredibly successful career as a well-known analyst and author. It is true that Neville does value the process of looking at one's past in order to understand the reasons one's life may have developed in a certain way. When taking all these factors into account, Neville's world view (Symington, 1996, 2016) declares that time and again, he pushes forward despite adversity; he seems to me to hold an Ironic world view. It could be said that his vision of reality represents a form of 'emotional bricolage'.

Conclusion

Neville Symington clearly experienced a sub-optimal attachment experience: I would suggest that his attachment schema is insecure ambivalent. However, it appears that he has surmounted this in his later years, and his long marriage to his second wife bears testimony to this. His time in "Yorkshire's concentration camp" (Symington, 2016, p. 31) was understandably experienced as a veritable trauma. After a bumpy start as an adult, he found an answer to his quest in life as an analyst. In his autobiography, he clearly acknowledges a time of mental illness:

he found that his analyst, John Klauber, telling him that he was very ill came as a massive relief that, at last, his state of mind had been acknowledged. Despite his early difficulties in life, in terms of both attachment and his time as an ordinand and priest, I think that Neville has always sought to make positive life's negative experiences. He seems to me to envisage life as sometimes Tragic, sometimes Ironic.

Chapter 6

The Life of Nina Coltart

Introduction

The book about Nina Coltart's life and dedication to her work as an analyst, *Her Hour Come Round at Last* (Rudnytsky and Preston, 2011), is essentially a series of recollections and tributes to Nina written by past analysands, supervisees, family and friends, plus readers and reviewers of her published writings. I found during my research it was exactly what I was looking for in terms of a treasure trove of views about her character and life.

I would like to begin by painting a picture of Nina's personality for you. A. H. Brafman, a friend, tells us that she had an irresistible smile, and her laughter was almost childish in its innocence (ibid, pp. 77–82). How charming! However, he points out that she had another distinct side to her character: she possessed an ability to become completely subsumed by a subject (a useful characteristic in a therapist!), and she was unwilling to suffer fools gladly (ibid, p. 77). He is absolutely definite about yet another aspect of her character that, in fact, I found mentioned time and again by different contributors. Privacy was seen by Nina as a right (ibid, p. 78). Her nephew, Martin Preston, makes the following statement: he talks about the way she developed an amazing sense of intimacy, yet at the same time, there was a sense of aloofness and the overriding need for privacy (ibid, p. 140). Gill Davies, who refers to Nina as her pen pal, makes a similar point about Nina's sense of privacy; she states that Nina disclosed little about herself to anyone; indeed, this dictum did not apply only to those in analysis with her. She tells us that it was difficult to discern whether Nina was happy or sad, interested or bored. In fact, various individuals point out with alacrity (as Brafman said) that Nina could cut to the quick if she sensed that someone lacked personal authenticity.

I find it illuminating that the reminiscences have been made by quite a collection of individuals with whom she entered into regular and animated correspondence. Gill Davies says she always looked forward to Nina's letters, recognising them instantly because of her unusual use of Conqueror paper (deep cream and dense, intense, like its user) and her easy-to-read, purposeful handwriting. Quite a number of her correspondents comment on how a feeling of pleasure and gratification accompanied the receipt of her regular missives; everyone comments upon

DOI: 10.4324/9781003316503-7

the speed with which she responded to their letters and her intuitive way with words.

However, Antonio Gransdon offers a comment that is extremely pertinent in helping us to decide if Nina was, indeed, a wounded healer. He knew her when both were students at Oxford together, but he notes that Nina was always the giver and he the receiver, which led him to feel somewhat guilty that she always took the role of the carer (ibid, p. 127). Friends such as Nina Fahri use the word 'vocation' (ibid, p. 86) to describe Nina Coltart's analytic work. This seems to me indicative of someone who is regarded as a wounded healer. Others are at pains to tell us that her earlier training as a doctor (at St. Bartholomew's Medical School) did not satisfy her pursuit of a vocation – both Nina herself and her nephew point out that she later realised that she had trained as a doctor as an identification with her deceased father, who had been a general practitioner; it simply performed the role of the bathwater. Fortunately, she did not make the mistake of throwing out the baby with the bathwater and instead went on to train as a psychoanalyst! This decision followed a suggestion made by a woman she met at a psychiatric hospital at which she was working. Nina had a long and illustrious career, gaining full membership of the British Psychoanalytic Society in 1969 and becoming a training analyst in 1972. However, three years before she died, she resigned from the society – a move which was greeted with some shock. Nina was, in fact, one of only three members to have done this in modern times. She left without regret, and describes her resignation and her retirement from practice as bringing with it a sense of freedom that was very welcome. It seems that she was devoted to her profession as an analyst but that when she felt the time was appropriate, she abandoned it with a sense of relief.

I think this almost brings my introduction to Nina's character to a conclusion. I would just like to relay the observation by Mary Nottidge, her goddaughter, that Nina declared that her idea of a perfect evening is to have close friends next door with all her favourite people enjoying a party, to which she has been warmly invited but which she actually declines to attend, and instead she stays home and reads a good book (Nottidge in Rudnytsky and Preston, 2011, p. 136). I think this statement is incredibly revealing. You may be like me and find, when I tell the story of her life, that it is this tension between intimacy and an abiding wish to maintain a distance that I find especially intriguing.

The Legacy of Nina's Childhood: A Traumatological Experience Leading to a Sub-Optimal Attachment Schema

Nina was born on November 27, 1927, the elder daughter of her parents, and lived for her first twelve years in Kent, where her father was a GP. She is survived by her sister, Gillian Preston, who still lives with her own family in Cornwall. Gillian has unselfishly given her time and energy to collaborate with Peter Rudnytsky to edit the volume about Nina's life to which I make reference.

There is ample evidence which enables us to appreciate that Nina suffered a number of traumatic incidents during her childhood and adolescence. No doubt this is another factor that leads me to define her as a wounded healer. Shortly before the Second World War, her parents bought a holiday property on the Lizard in Cornwall, and in 1940, they evacuated their daughters to live there in the care of Nina's beloved nanny (whom Nina described as her first love object). After some months, Gillian started to suffer from an undiagnosed illness (perhaps glandular fever), and the local doctor sent for her parents in order that her father could decide on his daughter's appropriate medical care. Her parents set off by rail, but tragically, the train on which they were travelling jackknifed, and several coaches were crushed. Nina and Gillian's parents never reached the station in Cornwall, where the girls were waiting, excitedly anticipating their arrival. Nina remembers waiting in vain for four hours and then being sent home without any explanation. It was only the following day that the girls were informed that they had lost their parents. Nina, in telling this story to Andrew Molino at an interview shortly before her death, in 1997, remembers that she was eleven at the time. In fact, she was actually almost thirteen. I guess that her memory reflects the fact that she felt that she was still very much a child when this dreadful turn of events overtook her. She rarely spoke about this tragedy to anyone; even the friends with whom she regularly corresponded were mostly unaware of her tragic loss in childhood. She spoke in *How to Survive as a Psychotherapist* (Coltart, 1993a, p. 101) about how she suffered from a psychopathology as a result of what she described as "a fracture" in her life story. This, she believed, led her to become a psychoanalyst. As a consequence of this tragic loss in childhood, Nina decided that she would never marry, and she also found the notion of having her own children even more abhorrent. She could not bear the thought that she might leave them as she had been left.

I assume that it was a function of this extreme sense of loss that the memoir to Nina, by Rudnytsky and Preston, is peppered with allusions to the way that she appreciated that she suffered from a passionate determination to remain separate, which could be registered as her being standoffish (Coltart, 1996b, p. 50).

However, Nina herself made it clear just a few years before her death that there was an antecedent to the "fracture" (as she called it). Her parents' untimely deaths in fact replicated feelings of abandonment that she had struggled with earlier in her childhood. She remembers her mother as depressed and anxious. I guess, in Andre Green's words, Nina's mother was a "dead mother" – physically present but emotionally absent (Green, 1983). It seems that Nina's own mother suffered from anxiety and depression as a result of not being the favoured child of her mother. Nina's uncle, the favoured child, had gone to war (WWI) and had managed to return unscathed, only to die very near to home in a motorbike accident shortly afterward. Nina's grandmother was inconsolable, and her retreat into depression grew more pronounced when, soon after her son's death, her comparatively young husband died suddenly as well.

In childhood, Nina felt that the role of "secure base" (Bowlby, 1988) was actually held by her beloved nanny rather than by her mother. However, fortune would have it that this nanny kept disappearing from her life, too, before returning, each time with no explanation or forewarning. This was in actuality because her nanny also functioned as a midwife in Nina's father's GP practice, and so Nanny would disappear at times to help some needy mother through her confinement. This fort/da rhythm was not happily assimilated by the young Nina, and so she was already struggling with the dark shadow of abandonment when her parents failed to arrive in Cornwall. The two sisters were rapidly despatched to the care of their grandmother, whom Nina described as a "wicked grandmother" (perhaps as in fairy tales!) who did not care for them in the compassionate manner which they so much needed at this time. Grandmother speedily arranged for her granddaughters to attend a highly regarded girls' boarding school in Sherborne. As Winnicott (1965) said, Nina and Gillian had already endured unthinkable trauma, but the girls were unfortunately consigned to endure a cumulative trauma.

Nina entered her training analysis with Eva Rosenfeld. The latter had in fact been persuaded to come out of retirement in order to see Nina because it was deemed that she was a good match for Nina. Rosenfeld, too, had suffered huge losses in her life: three of her four children had pre-deceased her, her daughter dying as the result of a mountaineering accident. Mrs Rosenfeld, in her turn, had been analysed by Melanie Klein, who had suffered the loss of her eldest daughter in a mountaineering accident also. In this way, it seems to me that Nina was enmeshed in a pronounced intergenerational trauma of loss. It is my guess that Mrs Rosenfeld was so traumatised by her own losses that this pain predominated in her countertransference to Nina. In consequence, it seems that Mrs Rosenfeld was not able to help Nina to work through her own fracture. My summation is that Nina would have been better served by a different choice of training analyst. It is no small wonder that Nina said that she would have liked a second analysis with Wilfred Bion. She may then have been able to work through the losses which, I guess, were at the root of her depression and anxiety.

In 1989, Nina joined the Institute of Group Analysis and attended lectures and group sessions there. Whilst there, what began as a soral transference to the facilitator developed into a maternal transference. She suffered her first experience of a full-blown panic attack during one session when she was appalled that 'her mother-analyst' did not rescue her or save her from her traumatised state; this was experienced as a repetition of her relationship with her real mother. She remained frightened by the experience.

The Heart of Nina's Psychopathology: The Agony of Waiting

I firmly believe that the answer to the root of Nina's psychopathology lies in the sentence that Nina uttered to Andrew Molino in 1997: she could not bear the anxiety of waiting for someone she loved and depended upon to come (Molino, 1997, in Rudnytsky and Preston, pp. 195–196).

It is little wonder, therefore, that Nina was such a stickler for punctuality. Neither is it perhaps surprising that she found the career of a psychoanalyst soothing to some extent: where else are one's clients so aware of the rigours of punctuality? As a psychoanalytic psychotherapist myself, I find the routine of the day ("Ah! It is 12.00 midday; it will be Susie knocking now") an antidote to anxiety.

Nina admitted to Molino in her interview with him shortly before her death that she was imbued with a sense of being 'special'. She felt that she knew more than other people as a result of her prolonged struggle with loss and abandonment. In consequence, she felt she was "superior" to those who had not suffered a fracture as she had (ibid, p. 192). I have found in my clinical career that this is not uncommon with those who have experienced a major trauma during their youth that effectively leads them to mature earlier than their peers or at the natural life stage. This sense of 'being special' provides evidence for the notion that Nina, indeed, was 'different from the norm'.

Her Hour Come Round at Last: The Moment at Which Nina Was Confronted With the Rough Beast

The title of the book from which I have been fortunate enough to glean so much detail about Nina Coltart has been mentioned previously: *Her Hour Come Round at Last*. It may fascinate you to know that the title is a reference to the underlying rationale for the title of her book, *Slouching Towards Bethlehem . . . and Further Psychoanalytic Explorations* (Coltart, 1993b). This concept of "slouching" is taken from Yeats's poem *The Second Coming*. In this, he describes the coming of the hour of the "beast" (sphinx-like: with the head of a man and body of a lion). An apt description of "the rough beast" in Nina's life story! I think it is true to say that Nina's hour cometh when she retired from practice. No longer was she able to exist as a result of an end to what I would define as the 'pseudo-intimacy' of her life as an analyst. Nina was mindful always that as therapists, we should not rush to too-hasty interpretations but need to be patient and allow the patient the time to come to the hour of his awakening: the point at which the rough beast cometh.

As I have indicated above, Nina's own 'rough beast' arrived when she decided to retire from clinical practice. It is my belief that her practice as a clinician provided her with the belief and feeling that she was, as she once said, "an expert on intimacy" (Rudnytsky and Preston, 2011, pp. 61–63). I think that the analytic sessions provided her with a sense of intimacy – but I also feel that because we as therapists purposefully do not disclose details about ourselves, this intimacy runs in one direction only in reality: it is not mutual. Indeed, we give no more or less than our whole selves – isn't this, as Rudnytsky says, what essentially makes us healers (Rudnytsky and Preston, 2011, p. 167)? However, I noted in Anne Powers's book about the appropriate time at which to retire from practice (Powers, 2016, p. 143) that one of her contributors talks about the "exquisite" nature of one's abstinence. It is true that we tend to follow the rule of abstinence, much as our patients may try all sorts of means in the transference to persuade us to give details about our lives. Personally, I have always found this abstinence less than exquisite. Not so for some therapists such as Nina, I suspect – she too found it exquisite, just as did Anne Powers's contributor. For me, the phrase that abstinence is exquisite is paradoxical. Personally, it costs me to maintain this abstinence. On the contrary, I think that Nina's patients provided her with a much-needed sense of replenishment because of the intimacy that she derived from interacting with them, but she need not reciprocate. This 'pseudo-intimacy' – which she mistook for true intimacy – was sadly missed, I suggest, when she retired from psychoanalysis. By the time she retired in 1994, Nina had realised that she no longer had the brilliantly accurate memory with which many of us as therapists are blessed. With failing health also, she did well to recognise that it was time to retire. However, she wrote to Mona Serenius (a correspondent from 1994 until Nina's death in 1997) that after suffering a perforated duodenal ulcer and an associated operation, she did not know how to feel fully sound again in herself (Rudnytsky and Preston, 2011, p. 107). I firmly believe that in finishing the provision of her analytic sessions with her patients, she lost her sense of purpose – what I term in this research 'her quest in life'. Her patients had, in fact, provided her with a feeling of being alive and not alone.

Now, with failing health as well as the loss of intimacy she had been able to gather from her daily encounters with patients, she was no longer able to envisage going on. She was suffering from significant health problems: crippling arthritis, osteoporosis, thyroid problems, an operation for a perforated duodenal ulcer and heart disease. I guess that the idea of being reliant upon others – waiting for her sister or other carers to arrive and look after her – was too much to bear, just as she had verbalised to Rudnytsky. In fact, her sister states in a short memoir, *A Five-Minute Introduction*, that she felt that Nina could not countenance the dependency that her illnesses would necessitate (ibid, p. 145).

Evidence of Mental Illness

Very sadly, on June 24, 1997, Nina Coltart took her own life with an overdose of sleeping pills. She left a note upon the door of her bungalow in Leighton Buzzard telling possible visitors that she did not want to be disturbed: she was having "an extra lie-in". Clearly, this was not a '*cri-de-coeur*' suicide attempt. She did not want to be found and saved from death. She had written previously (1993a, p. 45) that suicide is an act of failure, but I sincerely wonder if she contemplated her suicide in this manner. Rudnytsky says that suicide can be an act of freedom or an act of despair – or both simultaneously (Rudnytsky and Preston, 2011, p. 165). It is my belief that Nina decided to make the choice to finish her life both an act of freedom and an act of despair. In terms of despair, I think that Brendon MacCarthy encapsulates the tragedy of her passing in one simple sentence: "Undone by the pure agony of waiting" (ibid, p. 185). Nina could not countenance the inevitable times that would occur because of her deteriorating health when she would helplessly be forced to wait for help to arrive. The idea of this becoming a reality was anathema to Nina with her childhood memories of waiting interminably at that train station in Cornwall. This loss, I suspect, echoed the repeating mini-traumas of the times she would wait for her beloved nanny to return.

It seems to me that there are facts to indicate most definitely that Nina took her life with premeditation and after careful balancing of the alternatives. She wrote to her friend that *The Baby and the Bathwater* (1996b) would be the last book that she would write. Her friend and correspondent, Mona Serenius, wondered when she read this whether her friend was terminally ill but banished the thought. She had no idea of the devastating decision that I think Nina had probably already taken by that point. Nina did admit her frailty in saying to Mona that a friend was typing this last letter because the anti-depressant medication meant that she could no longer write. In similar vein, Gill Davies (Rudnytsky and Preston, 2011, p. 92) tells us that the last she heard from Nina was in the form of a postcard – an unusual method of communication – informing her that Nina was ill and dependent and would not be able to write again. Gill replied kindly, offering to visit, but was discouraged by Nina. She says that she knew that it would be appropriate to back off but did not think that Nina's life would end in such a dramatic way (ibid, p. 92).

Maybe Nina's final act of suicide is proof enough of mental disturbance – yet another theme which is a feature in the lives of 'wounded healers'. One can argue, however, that it was a cogent decision, taken by a woman who abhorred the idea of dependency – a sensible alternative to a living death. This depends upon one's own viewpoint. I believe that the decision to take one's life is not made when in sound mind. However, I think that there is ample other evidence to declare that Nina suffered in terms of mental health issues for most of her life, battling both crippling anxiety and depression. Nor do I think that this is, in reality, surprising, given the depth of her early trauma.

Nina's Tragic World View

The fact that she found a worthy cause to which to devote her life tells me, as a psychotherapist, that she did not deny that her early years had taken their toll. I think she was fully cognisant of the effect of that cataclysmic day in Corn-wall, but with a truly Tragic vision of reality, she accepted that the past cannot be undone and that some things are irredeemable. The fact that there is definite evidence that she took the decision to end her life in a premeditated fashion declares to me that she did not have an Ironic vision of reality. Had this been so, she would maybe have decided that there were other ways in which she could face the com-ing years of old age and failing health. Remember, the individual with an Ironic world view tends to look at the difficult hand of cards he or she has been dealt and looks for how he or she can best use those cards.

Nevertheless, Nina found a way of living a solitary life (her stated intention) yet paradoxically was able to find a sense of connection, both through her work as an analyst and through the assiduous manner in which she maintained her regular correspondence with her friends, ex-supervisees and ex-patients. I was at first puzzled to discover that she never met up with many of those friends in the flesh. When Mona Serenius, who lives in Sweden, suggested that they meet up in Oxford during her trip to Britain, this offer was declined – respectfully and kindly, but nevertheless declined. Nina stated that she thought that in so doing, they might spoil their friendship. This reminds me of the argument that it is unwise to ever meet with your patient socially, either during treatment or thereafter. I think a lot of people believe that one may well not appear to the patient as one does from the relative distance of the analysis, and this may compromise the vision of the internal object that makes the patient feel secure. Perhaps Nina had similar feelings regarding the friends with whom she corresponded.

"An Expert on Intimacy"?

It was Nina's belief that she was "an expert on intimacy" (ibid, p. 61), as she had once stated to a colleague at the Institute of Psychoanalysis. However, I would demur. If I were given the opportunity to reflect upon her life – as, indeed, I am now – I might ask: "Is this an accurate reflection of the reality?" It is accurate to say that Nina knew so well how to create an intimate environment in which the patient felt safe enough to share his or her innermost thoughts and feelings; the secrets in their life. However, as I have intimated earlier, the analytic *milieu* is a pseudo-intimate environment, precisely because one (as the therapist) does not participate in this intimacy through a process of mutual disclosure (the normal and essential way to deepen a friendship). Nina kept her distance, just as she also did in her correspondence with friends. As she declares in *Slouching Towards Bethlehem* (1993b, p. 110), one needs to remain both detached yet involved. She made the point that this is at the very root of our profession.

In fact, Nina's friend Janet Mothersill, with whom she was at primary school in Kent and later at Sherborne, never met with her in adult years. Janet plaintively states that she hoped to have the opportunity to meet up with Nina after her husband died in May 1997, but as Nina's death intervened, this did not prove possible. Jan Reid, also a friend at Sherborne, met with Nina every five years or so at her sister's house in Cornwall, although she somewhat tellingly makes the comment that she never lost a sense of awe with regard to Nina.

Nevertheless, if and when Nina did invest in someone wholeheartedly, she was distraught when she lost that person. Several contributors comment upon how close she was to an unnamed friend in the West country and that Nina was devastated when her friend developed lung cancer and died.

In similar vein, Nina seemed to be well aware (not surprisingly) what real loss involved. She commented to Maggie Schaedel (a supervisee and friend) that when one loses an analyst after one's analysis comes to an end, it is not a case of real, grief-ridden loss, because if the analysis is terminated successfully, the patient no longer really needs the analyst (Rudnytsky and Preston, 2011, p. 64).

It is accurate to state, however, that her enduring friendship meant a lot to many individuals. During her psychoanalytic training, she undertook an infant observation, and she kept in touch with Peter ("her baby") for all the years of her life, even donating five hundred pounds to help him with his post-graduate studies.

Ways in Which Nina Was 'Different From the Norm'

Nina differed from the majority in a number of ways. Firstly, as a psychoanalyst, a number of individuals comment upon the way that she had a power that others lacked. I found most moving the way that Alex Douglas-Morris (an analysand) envisaged Nina as a lighthouse – her 'light' shining the way so that each of her patients could find the way to their personal 'harbour'. Alex touchingly believes that Nina's 'light' continues to shine as bright, even though she has bodily passed away (ibid, p. 29). Clearly, he had internalised the object. Nina managed to retain the difficult balance between activity and silence, between engagement and distance. Another patient, Muriel Michieson Brown, was captivated by the way she perceived that her analyst enjoyed psychoanalysis with her – there always being a strong sense of being in it together (ibid, p. 21). Much as Nina was wedded to psychoanalysis, she felt that psychoanalytic theory is emotionally unfinished, that there is a great deal about human life that it has yet to encompass. Susan Budd (herself an analyst now but at one time an analysand of Nina's) makes the point that Nina recognised that what is most important is that one is a gifted therapist – it is not about whether one is neurotic oneself or can be more balanced in approach to life. Nina recognised that it may well be that it is the neurotic analyst who is able to understand the patient by a capacity to understand when less neurotic therapists find it impossible.

Lastly, with regard to Nina's approach to analysis, I want to recount her reaction to the University of Kent's response to her proposal to give the following title to her forthcoming lecture. She entitled it 'Blood, Shit and Tears' (as a 'nod' to Churchill's famous clause). She was met with looks askance at her publicising of the word 'shit'. She pronounced that she was simply amused by the puritanical tendencies of psychologists at that time. So – a sense of humour and a disregard for authority!

Indeed, I detected (during my coding and categorisation) that Nina shared this disregard for authority that proves to be in common with a number of the life stories I have researched. She evidenced a definite suspicion of authority (ibid, p. xxvii). Gill Davies, one of her publishers and a friend, commented that Nina's views were so unlike the many self-important writers who consider themselves to be high and mighty. Nina firmly disliked the stuffiness and rigidity of the analytic world (ibid, p. 23). As mentioned earlier, she was one of only three members of the British Psychoanalytical Society that has seen fit to resign in modern times. She was deeply hurt by the way in which the London Clinic of Psychoanalysis did not recognise and give credence to the dedication that she had showered upon it for more than a decade of her life.

I would like to venture another distinct way in which Nina differed from most, even within the psychoanalytical fraternity. She became renowned for taking pleasure in assessment of candidates regarding their suitability for analysis and was, in fact, known as a godmother in matching new patient to appropriate analyst (Pina Antimucci – supervisee) (ibid, pp. 43–58). She would carry out an assessment, recommend that the individual begin analysis, but ask them to wait until the answer of a 'match' would swim up from the unconscious. She carried out more than 3,000 assessments during her career! Personally, I think her choice to specialise in assessments was due to her ambivalence about the cost of true intimacy in relationships. Maybe she felt that full intimacy may bring too great a pain, from which she felt she would not survive a second time!

Conclusion

In the thirty years in which I have been immersed in the analytic world, I have always had a fondness for Nina Coltart. I think this dates from my reading the first draft published of her paper, *Slouching Towards Bethlehem . . . or Thinking the Unthinkable in Psychoanalysis* (Coltart, 1986): the paper was a precursor to the book of that name. This and her later book about how to survive as a psychotherapist, complete with the recommendation that one has a plastic wastepaper bin in one's consulting room "for vomit", appealed to my own more informal style and wry sense of humour. I agree with Nina Coltart that as a therapist, one must be real, approachable and warmly welcoming.

Having read this incredible book edited by Peter Rudnytsky and Nina's sister, Gillian Preston, I firmly believe that it was in Nina's capacity to find a way through life whilst simultaneously acknowledging the intractability of the past and its influence upon the present that she achieved so much acclaim. I was deeply saddened by her death, not least because the very month that she died, I had a date in my diary to make her acquaintance in real life at a seminar she was due to present.

Chapter 7

The Life of Sigmund Freud

Introduction

Sigmund Freud was born in 1856 in the little town of Pribor, near Freiburg in Moravia. At that time, Freiburg was part of the Austro-Hungarian Empire; nowadays, it is part of the Czech Republic. He was the eldest child of his father together with his father's second (possibly third) wife, Amalia Nathanson. As the eldest and a boy, Sigmund found favour with his parents. "Mein goldener Sissi", as he was called by his mother, was born in a caul; this was generally believed at the time to be a portent of greatness (Webster, 1995, p. 34). Sigmund would tell how it was believed that he was destined to achieve great things; indeed, he came top of his year six times out of eight whilst at the Gymnasium (senior school) (ibid, p. 35).

'Different From the Norm'

However, this is in stark contrast to his memory of his father's words to him after Sigmund, aged seven, had urinated in his parents' bedroom that "the boy will never amount to anything". What a blow this may have been to his early narcissism! However, I wonder if his father's very words echoed in Sigmund's mind and provided him with the motivation and ambition to succeed: maybe he thought to himself, "This child will definitely amount to something!" (Phillips, 2014, p. 49).

An example of his certainty that fame would come to him can be seen in the way he wrote from Paris to his fiancée, Martha Bernays, that he was intending to destroy all his private papers and notes (apart from family letters) in order to make the task more difficult when authors in the future wanted to write a biography about him. Twenty-nine at the time, Sigmund was yet to achieve any notoriety; he had yet to invent psychoanalysis; yet he was sure in his mind that he was destined for greatness, destined to become a hero of messianic proportions. Ernest Jones, who wrote the first (three-volume) biography of Freud, in fact censored certain episodes in Freud's life, as well as certain passages from his letters, in order to support the thesis that Freud was, indeed, a messiah (ibid, pp. 13–14). E. M. Thornton (1984; in Webster, 1995, p. 22) contends that many of Freud's

DOI: 10.4324/9781003316503-8

ideas were born whilst he was under the influence of cocaine, to which he was addicted for some time. Jones (1953, 1955, 1957) stops short of this, but nevertheless, it is the truth that Freud needed to use cocaine, which had been prescribed to ease the pain in his palate caused by a cancerous growth.

It seems to me that the young Sigmund's certainty that he was destined for messianic greatness explains in essence the way in which Freud was 'different from the norm': a theme that continually recurs in this research. I think that this unusually high level of self-assurance was a function of the favouritism that he received from his parents combined with a fierce determination that he would not suffer the crippling effects of poverty and disadvantage that his father and mother had endured. In fact, he was 'special' to his parents because he was the eldest and a boy, yet also at one and the same time he was 'not special' by virtue of the fact that his father had two older sons from his first marriage: Emanuel and Philipp. Maybe the existence of two step-brothers also motivated Sigmund's determination to achieve recognition. The expectations of greatness and favouritism showed to him by his parents were, in my opinion, something of a poisoned chalice. If there is a family myth that one is destined for greatness, then it is difficult to lead a normal life. Society at large is apt to 'knock' and undermine the reputation that public figures build up. This is even more true in today's media-driven society: one only needs to look at the life story of Diana, Princess of Wales, to see this process in action.

Evidencing a certain level of caution, Sigmund refrained from marrying Martha Bernays (even though they were affianced for over four years) until he felt that his status was such that he would be able to support her and a possible family with sufficient income. The couple married in 1886, and Martha rapidly gave birth to three daughters and three sons. It is reported that following the birth of the sixth child Martha, denied Freud 'his conjugal rights' so that there would be no more children. He is said to have bemoaned the fact that the marriage had become "amortised" (Freud/Jung Letters, 1908–1939, p. 94, in McGuire, 1974, p. 210.) He was also responsible for supporting his wife's sister, Minnie, who lived with the couple in order to provide his wife with adult company as a consequence of her husband's arduous work schedule and to help her run the household. Although the Freud family were not wealthy in the early years, they did have a number of servants to help with the chores and the child-rearing, as was typical in that era for middle-class members of society. There have been rumours that his life with his sister-in-law and his wife constituted a menage a trois, but I believe this to be nothing more than scandal-mongering amongst those who have sought to bring Freud into disrepute.

In the same year as he married, Freud set up in private practice as docent in neuropathology. At the same time, he also pursued his occupation as a university lecturer, which won him high status and was a rare position for a Jewish person to achieve. He was yet to invent the treatment process that became known as psychoanalysis. He set up in private practice following his study of medicine at the University of Vienna from 1873 to 1882. In 1885–1886, he spent six months in

Paris, studying the work of the famed neurologist Charcot, financed by a bursary from the University of Vienna. He was very much influenced by the illustrious Charcot and his method of hypnotising neurotic and hysterical patients in order to enable them to recall previously repressed memories. It is worth noting, that the very term 'repression', as applied to the psychological process involved, had not yet become common currency in our language. The term was popularised by Freud along with the many papers he published on his new method of treatment. Charcot was famed for his weekly demonstrations at *La Salpetriere* of hypnosis of patients, where he demonstrated to his students (and society in general that flocked to his lectures in order to see his method and the amazing effects).

Freud's Early Career

Consequently, when Sigmund Freud first set up in practice shortly after his time in Paris, he used hypnotism. At this stage of his career, he also used massage and prescribed various physical treatments such as spa baths and rest-cures. At this time, hysterical patients (predominantly female) were generally disregarded as malingerers and received little help from psychiatrists or neurologists. The fact that Freud gave hysterical individuals time and attention, taking their complaints seriously, was novel in itself. Gradually, he started to use the talking cure by commanding his subjects to remember whilst placing his hand firmly on the patient's forehead. This technique was a forerunner to his insistence on free association, whereby he was convinced that if a person was encouraged to say whatever occurred to them, without any form of censorship, then unconscious memories (maybe associated with feelings of shame and regret) would float to the surface. However, reading a verbatim report of Anna Guggenbuhl's therapy with Freud published by her granddaughter (Koellreuter, 2016), it seems that in actuality, Freud did not always adhere to free association. He is recorded as initiating ideas and making interpretations concerning the Oedipus complex and other theories with which he was obsessed at the time. This book seems to show that Freud 'trained' his patients to talk about childhood memories and sexual fantasies.

By 1896, Freud had begun to effect his cure via free association and had abandoned the prescription of physical methods to treat hysteria. It was in this year that Freud first stated that his method of treatment was to be called 'psychoanalysis'. The method began to achieve renown largely as a result of the Wednesday-evening meetings with his colleagues and followers in Vienna, when they met to further the aims of the psychoanalytical movement (as it was so-called). These meetings were inaugurated in 1902.

Difficulties in Intimacy

During his life, Freud appeared to continuously engage in ardent discussion concerning his theories with a string of men, each of whom he tended to idealise for a time. His first such relationship was with Josef Breuer; then with Wilhelm Fliess, to be followed by an intense association with the Swiss psychiatrist Carl Jung. His association with Jung came to a passionate end when the latter disagreed with his colleague's insistence that all patients' neuroses resulted from matters of sexuality. Freud had grown to name Jung as 'his son and heir' in psychoanalysis, most particularly because this would mean that his profession would not remain known as a Jewish, Viennese tradition. After his schism with Jung, Freud continued his inclination to collaborate with other of his male intimates similarly over time (Alfred Adler, Karl Abraham, Otto Frank, Sandor Ferenczi).

I find it interesting that Freud's preferred method of communication was via correspondence with whichever particular colleague he favoured at that time. In this respect, he resembled Nina Coltart, who was also an avid correspondent. As I have put forward in Chapter 6 concerning Nina Coltart's life, it is believed that this method of soliciting intimate contact is favoured by individuals such as Freud and Coltart because it effectively leads to a degree of what I would term 'intimacy at a distance'. There is evidence of a level of distrust of intimate relationships. One could also argue that Freud's inclusion of Minnie in his household indicates that he was avoiding true marital intimacy by placing another person between himself and his wife. Indeed, such a mechanism is frequently employed in order to subvert the intimacy of the couple when one of the individuals finds coupledom overwhelming and suffocating. Minnie did tend to be the person with whom Freud discussed his work and theories, whilst to his wife, he gave the task of managing the household.

Psychoanalysis Starts to Become Known

Freud wrote his first major work with Josef Breuer that earned him fame and repute in 1895 – *Studies on Hysteria* (Freud and Breuer, 1895). This book detailed the work of Breuer with the patient who is known as Anna O. Anna was diagnosed as a young hysteric who suffered a myriad of physical symptoms which were believed to stem from her psychological disturbance. When Breuer succeeded in helping Anna to recall the events which had brought her such internal conflict (concerning her relationship with her beloved father), she immediately ceased to suffer any more symptoms. Freud and Breuer gladly concluded that it was possible via talking to cure an individual of physical symptoms, putting forward the belief that such symptoms were in fact psychosomatic manifestations of intrapsychic conflict rather than having an organic cause. The two friends jubilantly recorded details of treatments which provided some proof of Freud's emerging method of treatment, but they neglected to recount the sequel to this story: Anna was later admitted to another clinic as a result of the re-emergence of her symptoms. In fact, more recent evidence suggests that Anna O was not an hysteric at all but was suffering from epilepsy. In those days, it was very difficult to diagnose epilepsy; this only became possible following the invention of the electroencephalogram (EEG) in the 1940s. I wonder whether this does not disprove Freud's method of treatment; could it be that Anna's symptoms re-emerged as the result of the relatively short period of analysis with Breuer? Indeed, the re-emergence of Anna's symptoms might be accounted for by the fact that Breuer ceased treating Anna abruptly when he realised that his wife had become very jealous and was becoming increasingly depressed in consequence. It is a fact that Freud's treatments were not as long term as we would recommend nowadays. For example, Anna Guggenbuhl (Koellreuter, 2016) only attended eighty sessions of analysis over a four-month period. One may thus wonder whether Freud's method lacked permanent 'cure' because he did not persevere for long enough. For example, Gustav Mahler's analysis with Freud consisted of very short analysis during a holiday that Freud took! Such diminutive consultations would be considered thoroughly insufficient in today's psychoanalysis or psychoanalytic psychotherapy.

Freud, by now, had taken to listening to his patients' stories by sitting behind them as they reclined on a couch (divan). Freud explains in one of his technique papers that the reason for this method is twofold – partly because he felt that his patients would be more inclined to unburden themselves about the nature of their underlying conflicts with their therapist out of eye contact and partly because Freud could not endure being stared at for eight hours a day (Freud, 1913, p. 134)! Perhaps it raises one's cynicism in view of the fact that Freud admits to such a pragmatic motivation for this method of working. I find it astounding that some of his commands have been copied so rigorously by practitioners, as if this represents the only way of achieving results, especially when one takes account of his reasoning. We have indeed copied this dictum about the position of the couch yet not the typical length of analysis. Does this stand up to scrutiny? Is it not more accurate to say that we have adopted certain tenets because it suits us and ignored others? Freud, in fact, declared that he himself was unorthodox – stating in this regard that measures need always to be taken with the interest of the patient uppermost in one's mind. It is true, for instance, that he arranged to feed the 'rat man' during a session. He declared in defence of his actions that the man was very hungry!

Quite soon after Freud's first major publication with Breuer of *Studies on Hysteria* (1895), *The Interpretation of Dreams* (1900) was published. Shortly after, he published the other works which were to put the new method of psychoanalysis on a firm footing – *Three Essays on the Theory of Sexuality* (1901a), *Jokes and Their Relation to the Unconscious* (1905) and *The Psychopathology of Everyday Life* (1901b). He was responsible for the publication of a prolific number of papers and books. I guess that many of you as readers are conversant with some or most, of his writing, which can be found today in the Standard Edition (Volumes I–XXIII).

During this first decade of the twentieth century, Freud began to achieve international acclaim. The International Psycho-Analytical Association's inaugural meeting took place in 1910, and in the year prior to this, Freud made his one and only trip (with Jung) to America to lecture at the Clark University in Worcester, Massachusetts.

In 1917, Freud discovered a growth on his palate which was finally diagnosed as cancer six years later in 1923. This cancer served to cause him great pain over the coming years, for which he was prescribed morphine and cocaine by his personal physician. Gradually, despite some surgery, it became difficult for him to speak and to eat, and indeed, the pain involved in speech moderated the way he ran analytic sessions during his last years in practice.

He suffered additional emotional distress when his favourite daughter, Sophie, died from influenza at the age of twenty-six in 1919 (Kahr, p. 190). As the author has stated elsewhere in this book and a previous book (Fear, 2017), no pain is as traumatic as when a child pre-deceases the parent. Even though I tend to adhere to an Ironic vision of reality, essentially meaning that I attempt to make a positive from a negative, this is one area in which most sufferers hardly ever are able to make the experience positive.

In 1938, Freud, with his family, being of Jewish origin, was forced to flee from Vienna in order to be saved from incarceration in a concentration camp and/or death. In fact, his sisters did perish in concentration camps. He relied heavily upon a very useful friendship with Maria Bonaparte to enable him to escape to London with all of his family and many of his possessions. Many Jews were forced to flee – if they could manage to escape at all – with no possessions whatsoever. The Jewish fraternity had never known a sense of permanence – their story was an enduring tale of migration. It is perhaps understandable therefore that those of Jewish ethnicity have always had great regard for jewellery and precious stones in particular, because these jewels can be sewn into the hems of their clothes when they are literally forced to flee. In this way, they can take at least a portion of their wealth with them. The book now turns to the matter of Freud's ethnicity in order to interpret its effect upon this leviathan among men.

The Impact of Freud's Ethnicity on His Life: His Personal Trauma

Freud was born into a Jewish family in Pribor, a little town in Moravia. The Jewish population accounted for a mere 3% of the town's population (130 inhabitants out of a population of 4,500). His father was impoverished, and when Sigmund was three and a half years old, his father's business as a wool merchant failed, and the family moved to Leipzig. They did not prosper there either, and a year later, they moved on to Vienna, probably in order to be nearer family upon whom they could rely for help. At times during Freud's childhood, adolescence and early adulthood, there were periods when the powerful men of Vienna clearly discriminated against the Jews; at other times (according to the feelings of the emperor or the ruling mayor), the rules against Jewish individuals were relaxed. The failed revolutions of 1848 had brought to the forefront the question of how to confront and deal with what was referred to as the 'national question'. In other words, where should those belonging to ethnic minority groups fit into society? There was also talk of the 'social question' – how should the Empire deal with the widespread poverty in the land? The Emperor Franz Josef gave the Jewish population full civic rights in 1849 – the year following the failed revolutions. This greatly helped the Jewish fraternity to cope with the sense of impermanence that they had suffered for centuries. Although the Jews formed a tiny proportion of the total Viennese community, a large percentage of those who attended university were Jewish. Jewish members of society were generally resented and aroused suspicion because many of them were bright enough to earn themselves education and fortune, and this brought with it envious attack. However, because they were a close-knit community, welded together by their religious customs and practices, they were able to rely upon kinsmen in times of trouble. They tended to trade for a living because they were not allowed entry to many of the professions.

The Jewish fraternity lived in ghettos, not only because many were reliant upon the help of family and friendship networks but also because they had no choice. They were in fact only allowed to dwell in certain areas of most cities. Take, for example, the fact that traditionally, the East End of London consisted of a large Jewish contingent. Historically, this was a function of them being denied access to wealthier, 'nicer' areas of the city because of racial prejudice. However, when any ethnic minority becomes visible (by proliferation of their numbers and influence) to those of mainstream ethnicities, that minority tends to be perceived as a threat.

How did this incipient and institutional racism affect Sigmund Freud? Firstly, he was determined to achieve more success and prosperity for his own family than his father had done. Another of Freud's advantages lay in the fact that he did not need to migrate (to London) until the very end of his life. This provided him with a sense of continuity and a familiarity with the people around him, on whom he could rely for help during the years that he developed the practice of psychoanalysis. He often referred to his many benefactors. Politics was not a matter in which Jewish members of society typically became involved; it is true to say that Freud himself was politically naïve. For example, he did not take the Nazi threat by Hitler seriously until it was almost too late.

However, at one stage, with one particular mayor in Vienna, Jewish individuals were refused entry to the university. Freud did attend university and qualify as a doctor but was denied entry to certain specialties of the medical profession because of his ethnicity. It may also be accurate to say that he may have made the decision to enter private practice because the route to promotion was effectively barred. It is a fact that he found it very difficult to achieve the status of professor, and this may well have been a function of his Jewish ethnicity.

He remembered all too well, at age ten to twelve, his father walking quietly along the street when another man (a gentile) purposefully knocked off his new fur cap, telling him that he did not belong here. His father told how he silently ignored the slight and, picking up his hat from the gutter, walked on with fortitude (Phillips, 2014, p. 49). I wonder if this story accounts for the fact that Freud was determined to achieve fame and notoriety so as not to be dismissed as his father had been. It is not the physical spoiling of a new hat – it is the intentional slight that matters and creates an enduring sense of not belonging for the individual. As Freud repeatedly said, the facts do not speak for themselves. One needs to interpret the meaning behind the facts. Such bullying behaviour affects one deeply, even, as seen here, affecting the next generation by the incident being recalled and repeated as part of a family myth. Freud has said that it is perhaps no bad thing that psychoanalysis was invented by a Jewish person but was not only for Jews, and this is one reason that he encouraged his link with Carl Jung. The fact that Freud was part of a micro-society that suffered such significant racism meant that he definitely suffered from early life trauma.

Was it in order to combat the incipient level of racism that was endemic in the nineteenth and twentieth centuries that Sigmund Freud was so determined from an early age to achieve greatness? If one regards the effect of racism from an Ironic perspective, then one can appreciate that whilst the racism was appalling, it nevertheless actually provided Freud with the impetus to achieve greatness. Not only did he turn something 'bad' into something 'good', but many of us who have chosen this profession have benefitted also! It is true that some of us thrive on adversity, finding fascination with ideas different from the norm. There seems to me to be a tendency for psychotherapists to be outsiders in some sort of way. We have only to look at the lives of Patrick Casement, Viktor Frankl and Neville Symington to appreciate the outsider status that they have lived with. Sigmund Freud, of course, represents one such example, too.

It is true, too, that members of his family have benefitted perhaps because of Sigmund's notoriety – and maybe because of their genetic endowment. Lucian Freud has been one of modern art's greatest painters, and his works of art sell for enormous sums. Clement Freud also achieved fame as an MP and in other guises. We must all be aware that Anna Freud, Sigmund's daughter, achieved fame and renown for her work in the field of psychoanalysis. Maybe she had the capacity to withstand and hold her own in the 'controversial discussions' with Melanie Klein as a direct result of being her father's child. Maybe, however, this legacy also gave her an arrogance, and this may have partially precipitated the eruption of such vitriol. The author is not fully conversant with the details of the controversial discussions, but it seems a fitting interpretation to say that Freud's legendary success has lived on.

It seems accurate to say that he was affected by early life events, some as a result of his ethnicity, some because of his parents' relative poverty and misfortune. Although Freud may well have turned the discrimination he encountered to good advantage, it nevertheless brought a significant trauma during his early years and served to alter his life course.

Freud admitted publicly that he was not a religious Jew (Phillips, 2014, p. 33). He associated himself with the values attached to the Enlightenment rather than the "superstition" and "mysticism" of religion. Jews' fear and anxiety concerning the constant threat of loss of all of one's possessions is perhaps one of the reasons that his theories were dominated by the subject of "loss" (ibid, p. 39). He focussed upon the concepts of mourning, the death drive, castration, penis envy, the Oedipus complex – all examples of loss. As a member of the Jewish sub-culture, he must have been constantly aware of the possibility of extinction.

Attachment Difficulties

In discussing Sigmund's early (and continuing) traumas, it also seems relevant at this point to discuss his attachment difficulties. I think there is sufficient evidence, shown from his decision to live alongside his sister-in-law and his frequent passionate relationships with men with whom he later ceased all contact, to indicate that Sigmund did have difficulties with regard to intimacy. Also, as explained earlier, Freud did not tend to pursue face-to-face intimacy but intimacy at one remove – mostly via frequent correspondence.

His intimacy difficulties may stem from having been the favoured child in a house full of younger siblings. As her eldest child, he certainly had to learn to share his mother's attentions as more siblings were born. Sigmund's birth was also followed by the birth of a brother (Julius) who died, so his mother may well have been immersed in grief for quite some time. He may well have been resented by some or all of his siblings for being his mother's favourite. It may be helpful also to remember that in the early days of his life, his two half brothers, Emanuel and Philipp (from his father's first marriage), were also living in the family group. He spoke in 1933 (in *New Introductory Lectures*, 1932–1936) of the way in which the eldest child is continually "dethroned" by the birth of siblings; it constitutes the loss of suckling but also of the full attention of the mother. Interestingly, his sister Anna made the remark that Sigmund was always provided with his own *Kabinett* (an office/desk wherein was housed the only oil lamp in the house so that Sigmund could always study) no matter how crowded the family setting. It seems as if he was treated in some ways as an elder and a better (Ruitenbeck, 1973, p. 141). It is accurate to state that Freud's mother had a new baby each year for four years after the family arrived in Vienna. One can imagine that maybe this founded a resentment in Sigmund.

Any one of these factors may well have created attachment difficulties for Sigmund as he was growing up. Indeed, when his beloved nursemaid was arrested (by virtue of his elder half brother, Philipp, accusing her of theft), Sigmund was inconsolable until his mother returned. It is thought that he believed his mother had been taken away to prison. I find it intriguing that this man who engaged voluntarily in self-analysis never sought to disconnect himself from his emotional attachment to his mother, who remained an important figure in his life until she died aged ninety-five in 1930. He never talked specifically of his relationship with her, with the exception of his own experience (below) of the Oedipus complex. For those of you who have an interest in Freud's invention of the Oedipus complex, you will be familiar with his famous words: "I have found, in my own case too, the phenomenon of being in love with my mother and jealous of my father, and I now consider it a universal event in early childhood" (Freud, 1950 [1892–1899]).

His statement that the Oedipus complex is ubiquitous is probably reliant upon his own self-analysis, within which he grew to realise that he too suffered a time when he loved his mother so much that he wanted to own her, and to be her partner, and that at the same time, he hated and reviled his father, and had murderous intent towards him. If this was so, then it is highly likely that he also found it difficult to share his beloved mother with his younger siblings. Maybe because he was the eldest child, he needed to grow up extremely quickly and become independent.

Freud's World View

Despite the fact that Freud devoted his whole adult life to the creation and dissemination of ideas about his new regime – psychoanalysis – he did not believe that he could achieve a 'cure' for the many individuals who sought his help. As he said in those now-famous words, the best we can do is to transform hysterical misery into ordinary human unhappiness (Phillips, 2014, p. 13). I think that in this famous statement, we find evidence that Freud firmly held a Tragic world view. In similar tragic and pessimistic vein, he believed that when one recounts one's childhood, one remembers and recalls one's memories in view of all the disappointments that one suffered, ways in which one felt let down or disregarded, or unloved. As evidenced by this statement, I agree that a life story represents a 'narrative' version of the truth rather than a recitation of historical truth. We need to be aware of this caveat when we listen to one's patients' tales of childhood abuse and unhappiness. Freud was greatly disapproving of biography because of the way in which the biographer was wont to put a particular slant on 'the truth'. Maybe he was so suspicious and hostile towards biography because the task of the psychoanalyst is reminiscent of this in some respects. Whereas children live their lives forward, biographers live the lives of their subjects backward (Phillips, 2014, p. 44). Both biographers and therapists interpret the truth; they effectively decide to follow one line of interpretation and dismiss another. Using the example that I have gathered facts about Freud from various sources, including from Phillips (2014) and Webster (1995) plus a number of his writings, it is pertinent to state once again how important it is to use different sources of information in order to minimise bias. One tends to wonder how much one's interpretations as a therapist (or as an author!) are influenced by one's own pathologies and neuroses. Freud's view of his patients' recitations of their childhood memories is, indeed, a cynical yet worthy approximation of reality. However, my research about Freud has produced evidence that he was an individual who took a Tragic view of reality.

Freud's belief centred on the idea that the past will always affect the individual and that the past is irredeemable. He sees the reality of this as inescapable. He believed that whilst undergoing therapy, the patient will develop a transference to the analyst that effectively repeats aspects of his relationship with his original attachment object. He stated this clearly in one of his technique papers (Freud, 1914). We are but products of our pasts. Again, this represents a Tragic view, as does his belief (stated earlier) that there is no hope of 'cure' despite all the efforts that the individual and his therapist invest in psychotherapy. No undisputed happy ending!

I make it clear to my patients that the best we can hope for is that they will be better equipped after therapy to deal with life's vicissitudes as they arise in the future. There will be more disappointments and heartache. However, I do believe that one learns through long-term therapy to come to terms with the misfortunes that one has suffered and thus avoid self-pity or a belief that nothing in life will lead to healing. Long-term therapy is definitely worthwhile, even if patients will always suffer from remnants of their pathology at times of stress in their lives. This puts forward an Ironic vision of reality. One accepts the dramas and failures of the past and regards them in such a way that one finds something by which one can benefit if at all possible. I am not at all sure that Freud shared such an Ironic vision of reality. However, Phillips (2014) is sure that Freud believed that although one suffers losses, one can recoup those losses in terms of gaining knowledge. Perhaps, if this was true of Freud, there was an Ironic tinge to his world view. However, it seems most likely that he assimilated a Tragic vision given his experience as a member of Jewish society, always feeling like "an outsider" (Phillips, 2014, p. 57).

Freud's Pursuit of a Quest

In his own words, Freud set out to find some answers to the riddles in the world (Freud, 1927, p. 253). He did not believe that he had any wish to relieve suffering, which seems to emanate from a Tragic vision of reality. Rather, he stated that he was greedy to gain knowledge. Such an assertion provides us with the evidence that Freud did not feel himself compelled to help others because of his own 'woundedness', but maybe he was sensitised to the wounds of others as a consequence of his own wounds. However, despite his application to the task of self-analysis, he overlooked a number of episodes in his life that, had he sought to interpret, would, I suggest, have provided him with a greater degree of self-awareness.

Conclusion

It is my opinion that Freud was a wounded individual. This was in part as a result of sibling rivalry caused by having five siblings and two half brothers. It may well be that his share of his mother's attentions was too sparse for comfort. Also, the ambivalence regarding his role as the eldest and favourite probably left its mark. Undeniably, it is part of the reason for his immense level of ambition and determination to succeed at whatever endeavour to which he set his mind. However, there are traces of arrogance in much of his writings. I find this irritating and unattractive – perhaps because it is a quality that I have myself but have worked hard to eradicate.

At the beginning of this section, it is stated that Freud was always hungry for knowledge. It seems that he shared a feature in common with many of us as therapists. I have had a lifelong devotion to try 'to find out what makes people tick'. This is surely similar to wanting to solve some riddles of the human being's existence.

However, I was astounded to hear that Freud stated to Ferenczi that their patients were "rabble", suitable only to fund their livings and to enable them to learn more about their theories of psychoanalysis (Ferenczi, 1932, pp. 185–186). He also admitted to Weiss that only a minority of their patients were worth the effort they put into their patients' analyses (Weiss, 1991, p. 37 in Koellreuter, 2016, p. 94). All these thoughts of Freud – which could be, I recognise but feel should not be, disregarded as envious attacks by biographers – imply that Freud at least became disenchanted with helping his patients during the latter years of his career. It may well be that his thirst for knowledge proved to be a greater motivation to him than his desire to help the 'wounded soul'. It may well be that the pain and disability caused by his cancer led to a disenchantment with life and with the practice of analysis in particular.

Chapter 8

The Life of Viktor Frankl

The Basis of Frankl's Attachment Schema

It seems that Viktor Frankl – unlike so many – did not suffer difficulties in attachment terms during the childhood years of his life. It is pertinent that he was, in fact, very securely attached to his parents and his home life with them. During his early adult years as a medical professional, he was often required to stay overnight in the hospitals in which he worked, and interestingly, he expressed the need to return home for at least a night every week. It seems he mourned the daily sense of security derived from the familiarity of his family home. Maybe this is one of the reasons that despite finding fame and fortune in the mature years of his life, he failed to fulfil all three of his childhood wishes to: (a) own an automobile, (b) own his own house and (c) go mountain climbing. In fact, he succeeded in his desire to own a car and to climb mountains in his spare time (a life-long passion), but he never owned a house. Maybe this is a function of his being very attached to his parental home, which he was extremely upset to find, on his liberation from the concentration camps, to have been razed to the ground. Later on, he made a home with his second wife, Elly, in a rented apartment at No. 1 *Mariannen Strasse* in Vienna, where he resided for many years. Perhaps, when he had recaptured the sense of peace and safety once again, he could not bear to put this feeling in jeopardy by buying a different property.

In early adulthood, he remained very attached to his parents and was fiercely loyal to them. At the beginning of the Second World War, by virtue of his profession as a doctor, he was granted a visa to emigrate to America, but this posed a conundrum for him. He spent a whole day wandering the streets of the city of Vienna, wondering whether or not to take up the visa. As a Jew, if he escaped Vienna, he would not suffer the otherwise almost certain fate of incarceration in a concentration camp. However, whilst the idea of freedom was naturally very appealing, he was aware that if he left the country, his parents would immediately be transported to a concentration camp. His role as a psychiatrist in the *Policlinic* provided the effective insurance that gave his family protection from immediate transportation to the camps. He returned home from his day of wandering the streets still uncertain of his decision. Would God not give him a sign? When he

DOI: 10.4324/9781003316503-9

walked into the living area, he found his father clutching a tiny piece of marble. He asked his father what he was fingering. The reply came. In fact, the sliver of marble was a remnant of the building of the local synagogue, which had recently been destroyed by the Nazis. His father told him that he knew the precise location of the piece of marble in the synagogue. Viktor asked him to explain. The answer: it had inscribed on it one letter from the Commandments. It must be from a particular commandment because that letter only appears once in the whole of the commandments. Pertinently, Viktor asked his father for the identity of the commandment. "Honour thy mother and thy father". Viktor took this to be a sign – an omen which provided him with an answer to his conundrum. Consequently, he did not take up the visa.

He did not escape his fate as prescribed by the Nazis. For a short while, the family continued to live in their home in Vienna. However, it was not long before the dreaded knock on the door by the Nazi S.S. which ensured that the family were destined for incarceration in the concentration camps. They travelled by train, in carriages where there were so many people that the daylight only permeated the coaches through the very upper windows. Eventually, in Bavaria, the train came to a standstill. The ominous sign "*Auschwitz*" came into view.

A Bit 'Different From the Norm'?

Even during the first day of life in the camp, Viktor evidenced a determination to survive. In front of Dr Mengele each new prisoner was instructed to go either to the right or left. Mengele gestured that Viktor should go to the left. Behind his back, Viktor shifted queues – in actuality, the left-hand queue led straight to the gas chambers. This proved to be a beginning to a sequence of events in which Viktor's determination to survive saved him from extinction.

Frankl suffered from extreme exhaustion from the interminable task given to inmates: digging railway lines. He also suffered from overwhelming hunger. On one occasion, he was given some 'premium coupons' for special work completed. He was the proud possessor of coupons entitling him to twelve cigarettes. In fact, he exchanged the cigarettes for twelve soups. The soups, with just a 'whiff of meat' in them, helped to save him from starvation. He recalled scratching in the bare earth for a stub of raw carrot that he caught sight of amid the mud and detritus between the huts.

Frankl described how the Nazis purposefully sought to destroy one's sense of identity. For example, the prison guards purposefully forced the prisoners to divest themselves of all their belongings; this often included one's own coat and shoes, to be replaced by an inferior coat and shoes from someone else whose life had been terminated: a process of depersonalisation. When the prisoners first arrived at a camp, they were forced to strip naked and were shaved of all their hair, both on head and body. All of these mechanisms were carried out specifically to remove one's sense of dignity and personhood. A living death.

Frankl had foreseen his removal to the concentration camps. Consequently, he had sewed the manuscript of his book, *The Doctor and the Patient*, into the lining of his coat. When forced to give up his coat, he pleaded with the guard to be able to retain the manuscript – he was greeted with howls of derision at the naivety of his entreaty.

It was here, during his three years of incarceration, that Frankl's own personal experience of trauma occurred. However, the experience also gave something to him: he learned by experience how to cope with unavoidable suffering and to survive nevertheless. Having learned that one must never allow a camp guard to detect any physical sense of weakness or illness – for it would surely lead directly to the gas chambers – Frankl learned some lessons that were even more profound. He looked on as fellow prisoners lost the will to live – they would refuse to get up for duties in the morning and would stare unseeingly, catatonically into space. They would be seen to purposefully take out their last cigarette from a hidden place and proceed to smoke it; within a day, they would be dead.

Frankl's Quest

Frankl learned the sad, awful but profound truth that one was most likely to survive if one possessed a psychological meaning to life. It was whilst here in the camps that Frankl developed and honed his practical application of logotherapy. In order to hope to stay alive (the statistical chance was actually twenty-eight to one), it was of paramount importance to love something or somebody enough to feel that one would one day in the future be reunited with them or for the person to believe that it was imperative to achieve something before one's demise. Frankl was aware that both of the lives of his parents had been extinguished whilst in the camps; however, he did not hear about the fate of his wife (Tilly) until he was liberated from the camps and had returned to Vienna. It was there that he learned that she tragically died – one of 17,000 – from starvation and exhaustion after the Allies liberated the camps. Another 17,000 had died in that camp during the war. Frankl was able to survive because he felt that he must be able to rewrite his lost manuscript and publish it. A friend of his in the camp stole some S.S. forms from the offices where he worked. Another comrade gave Frankl the stub of a pencil as a precious birthday present. Armed with these gifts, he spent the long nights, avoiding cardiovascular collapse whilst suffering the effects of typhus, by making notes that would enable him in the future to rewrite his book. It suggests that this sense of purpose kept Frankl alive during the tortuous three-year existence. He understood that it is not a case of what we as individuals expect from life – instead, it matters what life expects from us.

He learned – as he exhorts the patient who enters logotherapy – the 'Third Viennese School of Psychotherapy' – (*Man's Search for Meaning*, Frankl, 2004) – that there are three factors which maintain the feeling that life is worth living and keep a person alive: a belief that one needs to stay alive to achieve a certain act; a determination to be reunited with another particular individual; and the finding of a meaning for unavoidable suffering.

In fact, there is evidence that supports the basic tenet of Frankl's logotherapy (the translation of 'logos' in Greek is the word 'meaning'). In some research, 78% of a sample of almost 8,000 students said that their first goal in life was to "find meaning and purpose in life". Another survey showed that 61% of individuals stated that there was someone that meant so much to them that they would be prepared to die for them if necessary. Individuals are seen to suffer from what we know as 'existential frustration' whilst they search to find meaning in life. This existential frustration is not seen as either pathogenic or pathological. It involves a tension – a struggle and a striving to find a purposeful goal. This belief in logotherapy is opposite to Freud's belief that pathology is the result of internal conflict – a tension between the drives of the ego and the id. It seems that Frankl's belief that we struggle to find a purpose in life and are more satisfied when we have found that sense of purpose explains why so many individuals find an answer to their quest in life by becoming a therapist. It seems sensible to suggest that Viktor Frankl found an answer to his personal quest by the invention and dissemination of the ideas of logotherapy and by his publication of *Man's Search for Meaning* (Frankl, 2004). It also seems that his personal gruelling experience in the concentration camps provided him with the evidence that logotherapy actually works in that it enables one to endure unavoidable suffering. It is not that Frankl advocates unnecessary suffering. Indeed, he states that unnecessary suffering is masochistic rather than heroic (Frankl, 2000, p. 117), but the reality is that a great deal of suffering is unavoidable, and given the right attitude, it is possible to convert personal tragedy into personal triumph. This leads one to an essential element of logotherapy: the capacity to self-transcend. This necessitates that one thinks and acts beyond one's own interests for the good of others. It is clear that Viktor Frankl personally behaved in this way during his years in the camps.

An Ironic World View

Next, we come to the matter of Viktor Frankl's vision of reality. For those of you who are well versed with the tenets of each of the world views, it will be rightly apparent that Frankl's vision was undeniably Ironic. He was able to make something positive from the most negative of circumstances. There could not be a greater crusher of the human spirit than life in the concentration camps of Nazi Germany. Despite the cruelty practised by the S.S. guards, Frankl managed to retain an inner locus of responsibility and control. He found meaning in life in spite of living daily in extremis. Undeniably, he was a wounded healer. And this analysis is made despite the fact that I have yet to take into account the way in which Frankl's early years – just like those of Freud – were punctured by the rabid anti-Semitism prevalent in those decades before the Second World War. The experience of belonging to a despised ethnic minority must have shaped the emerging spirit of life's great thinkers, such as Freud and Frankl. The fact that Viktor Frankl thought about the mysteries of life – the existential question – in such a novel way tells us that, in his very essence, Frankl was 'a bit different from the norm'.

Frankl agreed with Nietzsche's dictum of "That which does not kill me, makes me stronger" (Frankl, 2000, p. 89). Man needs to learn that he is responsible for himself. He is responsible for what he makes out of a situation of which he finds himself to be a part. Sometimes, what is required is to simply accept one's fate (even if that is not that simple!). Sometimes, Frankl argued, it is man's destiny to suffer – what matters is how one bears that suffering. It is also worth bearing in mind that one's past cannot be undone. It is irreplaceable and irrefutable. It can be helpful and positive to believe that what one has experienced cannot be taken away. With the realisation that in fact no person can be replaced, one can also come to see that it is a personal imperative that each of us should strive to go on existing. It seems a useful notion to take into account if an individual is contemplating suicide. Unfortunately, the mental state of such a person is unstable at such a time.

I have described a few of Viktor Frankl's experiences in the concentration camps and how, despite all the odds, Frankl grew from that experience. That is not to say that it was good for anyone to be forced to bear such an experience, but it seems Frankl used it to learn about the nature of life and suffering, and furthermore, it provided him with the opportunity to put his theory into practice. It seems that in telling some of the story of his experience in the camps, I have attempted also to explain some of the rudiments of logotherapy – the therapy he devised in the years thereafter and lectured on throughout the world until his death in 1997. His book, *Man's Search for Meaning* (Frankl, 2004), has been published in twenty-four countries, and the English version alone has sold nine million copies. The determination to disseminate his ideas about life provided him with a meaning to his life and gave him the courage to endure and survive the inescapable awfulness of his years in the camps. It seems that his life experience put his theory about life to the ultimate test. Certainly, he thought beyond himself: he gave his father his only phial of morphine that he had smuggled into the camps in order that his father did not suffer agony when dying from pulmonary oedema. In consequence, he knew that he had done his best for his father. He did not consider that it might be advantageous to keep it for himself.

A Period of Mental Illness

After liberation, he fought his way back to Vienna, his hometown. As he walked towards his old parental home, he found that the houses had been razed to the ground. During the days after his release, he also discovered that his first wife, Tilly, had died. He had lost his mother, father, brother and wife. Potzl, a senior colleague and friend in the hospital where he worked, feared for Frankl's life in the months after he had learned of such great losses. He describes how Frankl would cry inconsolably. Frankl certainly became familiar with a time of mental illness – another theme that I have detected in the lives of most therapists with a sense of 'woundedness'.

Conclusion

Victor Frankl undoubtedly suffered a traumatic time in early adulthood. He lost so many of his loved ones that undoubtedly he may have suffered from a sub-optimal attachment schema, yet it needs to be said that he enjoyed a long and secure relationship with his second wife. His early life seemed to be good in attachment terms, yet one wonders why he found it difficult as an adult to be away from his home for long. I wonder if, like Patrick Casement, he found security in structures as well as people. I put this idea forward because of his devastation at seeing that his family home had been razed to the ground. As stated earlier, he never achieved his aim of owning his own house, and it may be so because he became so attached to his apartment at No. 1 *Mariannenstrasse* in Vienna. He certainly seems to have suffered a period of mental disturbance following his release from the camp and his heartbreak at finding that both his parents and his wife had perished.

He undoubtedly held an Ironic vision of reality because the central tenet of his first book was the capacity of the individual to transcend his or her suffering, to turn the coin over and see how one can take something positive from the negative. His determination to devise and put forward the Third Viennese School of Psychoanalysis, i.e. logotherapy, tells us that this answered his quest in life.

Chapter 9

The Life of Carl Jung

Introduction

Carl Jung was born in 1875 to a poor couple in Kesswil, a little village in Switzerland. His parents were both the thirteenth child in their families of origin, so their marriage was regarded as an auspicious occasion. This is just one simple example of the way in which Swiss society was forever fearful yet respectful of omens (Bair, 2004, p. 7). It is probable that his parents were very loving towards Carl, given that he was actually their fourth child. Emilie had previously suffered two stillbirth daughters and a son who had only survived for five days. Happily, their fourth child was robust from the very beginning of his life (ibid, p. 19).

When Carl was just six months old, the family moved to Laufen when his father was granted a better living as a parish priest. Later in Carl's childhood, the family moved to Kleinhuningen, near Basel. This pleased his mother because it meant that she could be near her family, who lived in the Basel region. Carl's mother, Emilie (Preiswerk), came from a family enmeshed in the occult, and when they moved to Kleinhuningen, Carl too became very aware of the occult and what he called his mother's second personality (Jung and Jaffe, 2019, pp. 67, 69). His mother worked in the local peasant community as a seer, and she and her son attended seances regularly. The occult became an integral part of Carl's everyday life, and in fact, he was so enthusiastic about it that he chose to write his doctoral thesis on the occult. His first paper when he was admitted to Zurich's University's highly prestigious Zofingia group was entitled *The Border Zones of Exact Science*. He spoke of how his Preiswerk family were involved in the occult, and of himself, he said he had been born to ever behave as his black character insisted upon (Jung, Zofingia Lectures in Bair, 2004, p. 45). The paper posed the question that the occult and religious doctrines were a part of science. This early influence no doubt foretold the belief systems and the theories he promulgated during his later life as a psychoanalyst. Carl developed unusual beliefs regarding religion and says in his autobiography that if he had lived in the Middle Ages, he would have been burned as a heretic (Jung and Jaffe, 2019, p. 7) because of his belief in the occult and his secret distrust of God. He described himself as "an anti-Christ" during his adult years.

DOI: 10.4324/9781003316503-10

Carl was dimly aware that there were problems in his parents' marriage, and he says in *Memories, Dreams, Reflections* that his mother spent several months in a hospital and that he assumed that this was as a consequence of the difficulties in his parents' marriage (ibid, p. 21). It is actually thought that she was admitted on a number of occasions to a sanatorium, suffering from psychosis. Carl admits that he was deeply troubled by her absences. His father would repeatedly tell him that his mother loved him, and so he grew to associate the word 'love' with abandonment and a feeling of insecurity (Bair, 2004, p. 21). Consequently, he associated women with a feeling of unreliability, whilst he thought of men in terms of reliability but of powerlessness as well (ibid, p. 21). Consequently, as the young Carl grew up, it was his father that served as his primary attachment object. Indeed, his father was effectively responsible for raising Carl, with the help of a maid, of whom Carl said that she did not belong to the family, only to him (Bair, 2004, p. 21; Jung and Jaffe, 2019, p. 21). His parents slept in separate bedrooms, and as Carl suffered so much from insecurity, he slept in the same bed as his father until he left home to go to university. Carl found as he became adult, he was very sceptical of his father's religious beliefs and understanding of God (Bair, 2004, p. 64), and he believed his father was disappointed and disenchanted by his role as a parish priest.

Carl's Attachment Difficulties

The young Carl suffered various psychosomatic illnesses whenever he was separated from his mother. The first of these was at age three (in 1878). He came to understand that his illnesses were often a somatisation as a result of his mother's temporary absences from home. Illnesses included 'influenza', severe eczema and frequent gastric upsets. These psychosomatic symptoms – physical manifestations of his insecure attachment schema – continued throughout his adult life; periods of his parents' marital disharmony frequently led to periods of digestive illness and bouts of 'influenza' for Carl. He continued to suffer from bouts of influenza and gastric upsets as an adult, especially after the three occasions when his wife threatened divorce. After his split from Freud, he effectively suffered a complete breakdown of his mental and physical health that lasted several years.

He described his mother as a good mother, being physically stout and gay in manner, a good listener and possessing an excellent sense of humour (Jung and Jaffe, 2019, p. 66–70). It appears that she became a lot happier at Kleinuningen after his sister, Trudi, was born (Bair, 2004, p. 27), and she was once again in close contact with the extended Preiswerk family. Carl also expressed that at a young age, he became his mother's confidante and that she talked to him as if he was an adult (Jung and Jaffe, 2019, p. 70). Perhaps, therefore, there was an aspect of parentification in their relationship, which is not at all unusual in a child with an insecure ambivalent attachment schema. The parent does not protect and care for the child; the child provides the care for the parent. His mother usually behaved normally during the day, but at night, he describes her as becoming "uncanny". He described her as having two personalities – the one innocent, the other "uncanny" (ibid, p. 67).

As a child and adolescent, Carl spent most of his time in unendurable isolation. Maybe his secrets, by which he set great store, were a function of this isolation. He never shared some of his secrets with another living soul during his entire life. One of his secrets involved an important dream, in which he descended to a subterranean room, at which entrance hung a heavy green brocade curtain. He saw before him a giant throne on which stood a massive, fifteen-feet-high tower consisting of skin and naked flesh topped by an unseeing eye. In the dream, his mother exclaimed to him, "Yes, this is the man-eater!" Over the next years, he continuously asked himself whether his mother had said, "Yes, *this* is the man-eater" or "This is the *man*-eater". The central meaning of the sentence varies according to the emphasis. He came to realise as he grew up that the tower signi-fied a giant phallus.

Yet another 'secret' concerned a manikin. He carved this two-inch little man from the end of a ruler, giving the manikin a top hat and a frock coat made from a piece of wool. He then made the manikin a comfortable bed in a wooden pencil case, giving him a painted stone as a talisman, just as he himself found a great sense of security from a stone on which he sometimes sat. He hid the manikin in the attic at the top of the house, which he was actually forbidden to enter. He took great comfort from going to touch this manikin when he felt insecure and unwor-thy (Bair, 2004, pp. 28–29; Jung and Jaffe, 2019, pp. 34–37).

The stone, mentioned earlier, constituted another of Carl's secrets. He found it comforting to sit on a particular stone in the garden, allowing himself to think that the stone and he had an interactive relationship. He would wonder whether he was the person sitting on the stone or whether the stone itself believed that someone was sitting on it. Again, he records that this sitting on the stone stilled his feelings of conflict (Bair, 2004, p. 28; Jung and Jaffe, 2019, p. 60). It seems to me that his secrets were a reaction formation emanating from his feelings of insecurity.

His insecure ambivalent attachment schema as a result of his unusual upbringing became evident in his relationship with Emma Rausenbach, who was to become his wife. When he first set eyes upon the young heiress of fourteen (from one of the richest and highest-status families in Switzerland), he was certain that this was the girl he wanted to marry. However, it is debatable whether he met Emma when she was fourteen, as he recalled in his autobiography, *Memories, Dreams, Reflections* (Jung and Jaffe, 2019). Emma, on the contrary, let it be known that she met Carl when she was seventeen, shortly after she returned from finishing school in Paris. Emma refused Jung's first proposal of marriage for a number of reasons: primarily because she was engaged to a son of one of her father's busi-ness colleagues; partly because she disliked Carl's particularly loud and rumbus-tious manner; she was also aware that he had no money, nor was he ever destined to be wealthy, as he had decided upon a career as an *irrenarzt* (a psychiatrist). In the society of the time, this profession was regarded as the lowliest branch of medicine; psychiatry had only become a recognised discipline in 1888, just ten years before Carl chose it as his specialty. At first at university, he had thought he would specialise in internal medicine, but he could not afford the extra years as a student that this would entail, so he chose psychiatry because of his burgeoning interest in the individual's psychic life.

Emma, however, accepted Carl's second proposal of marriage. It is unlikely that a man as arrogant as Carl would have persisted with his entreaties had it not been that he had met his future mother-in-law when he was but a child (Jung and Jaffe, 2019, p. 22). She had taken care of him during one of his mother's absences. When Carl was a young man pursuing Emma, Bertha arranged to meet him in a café in Zurich, where she encouraged him to persevere in his approach to her daughter. This may also have been because Carl's mother and Bertha had attended the same school in childhood. Alternatively, she may also have encouraged the match because Bertha had married into a renowned and respected family with huge business interests, yet she too began life as a peasant.

The young adolescent Carl describes himself as suffering from a split personality, though he was careful to add that he should not be labelled psychotic in psychiatric terms (though he did suffer one schizophrenic episode that his followers called "his creative illness" whilst at *Chateau d'Oex* during the First World War). Carl himself came to name these splits Personality Number One and Personality Number Two. When he inhabited Personality Number Two, he was arrogant, loud, supercilious, overly confident, yet determined to display an acknowledgement of his peasant beginnings, appreciative of the natural world. He believed this personality to be his true self. However, when inhabiting Personality Number One, he would feel extremely insecure; tending to choose long periods of solitude, very much clamouring for the reassurance from his wife, whom he loved, cherished and valued (ibid, pp. 61–64). When Emma first knew Carl, she was only aware of Personality Number Two, and in consequence was perplexed by the fact that he sought constant reassurance of her love and that he remained determined to marry her despite her initial rejection. His insecurity regarding Emma's love in their early years together grew larger because their engagement was kept secret for quite some time in order that her father could gradually grow to accept the fact that his elder daughter was intent upon marrying Carl Jung, a peasant.

Carl had attended university in Zurich at the age of eighteen in order to study medicine. He was painfully ashamed of the poverty in which he had grown up. He hated the fact that he only possessed two shirts and one pair of trousers and had holes in his shoes and no socks when he attended the Gymnasium (ibid, p. 41). Neither was he familiar with the High German that was spoken at school and at university. The disadvantage of being the son of a poor parish priest, which he grew to appreciate when he began to attend the unfamiliar senior school, meant that he became determined to achieve a professional status and a good income in his adult life. Whilst at university, he felt that an abyss was growing between he and his father. This distressed him considerably. As one of the subjects of my research, his life story exemplifies how an individual's emotional development is affected by the rare experience of 'merging' with his father. When one has experienced a merged relationship during one's formative years, one tends to try to replicate this feeling in adult life. This may have been true in Carl's case. This may partially explain Carl's motivation to work as a therapist, where the therapeutic relationship becomes emotionally intimate between patient and therapist.

Before Carl met Emma, his father became ill with an unspecified illness and literally wasted away, dying several months later. Carl would describe how he carried his father from room to room and into the garden, his father nothing more than a bag of bones. This experience was felt by Carl to be an intense tragedy: he witnessed his emaciated father withering away before his very eyes.

The loss of his revered father did nothing to help Carl's insecure attachment schema, which had originated as a result of his mother's absences from home. This insecurity was to perpetuate throughout his life, persisting throughout his long marriage to Emma. Their marriage was not an easy one: Carl was in fact polyamorous; he considered it acceptable that he could take lovers, despite the fact that he wanted to remain married to Emma. Freud tried to disabuse him of this idea when Jung confided in him during their years of collaboration and friendship. In the early years of marriage, Emma learned to accept that Carl suffered from what she referred to as "compulsive infatuations" (Bair, 2004, p. 120). However, when he took on Sabina Spielrein as a patient, his infatuation with her extended beyond her sojourn as one of the four hundred patients at the Burgholzhi Hospital (the mental institution in Zurich where Carl was employed). From the first, sessions between Carl and Spielrein sometimes lasted over three hours. Later on, Sabina became a private patient, and later still went on to undertake research for him before training as an analyst herself. Sabina and he spent many hours closeted together, but he sought to disabuse Freud of the notion that anything improper had taken place with Spielrein. Meanwhile, she let it be publicly known that Carl refused to father her baby (it has never been proven that the two ever had sexual congress) (Bair, 2004, pp. 151–152, 154–157). Furthermore, she told her mother that the pair were in love (Freud/Jung Letters: McGuire, 1974, p. 210). Carl adamantly refuted this, and her mother insisted that he send her a report on his treatment of her daughter. Later, Sabina's mother wrote eight rambling letters to Freud to put forward her version of the relationship. Freud tried to pass the matter off as a function of the transference. Someone had sent Frau Spielrein an anonymous letter saying that Dr Jung was ruining her daughter. It is thought that Emma, Carl's wife, may have been the author of this missive.

Carl went on to have a number of affairs – and furthermore, carried these out in public, which scandalised the bourgeois society in which he moved. He proceeded to have a second very close relationship, for many years, with another female – Toni (Antonia) Wolff. He originally met her, too, as a patient, but he gradually introduced Toni into his family's private life. In fact, even his children grew resentful of the fact that they were forced to accept Toni's constant presence in their house and were furthermore instructed by their father to address her as "*Tante 'Toni*" (Dunne, 2015, pp. 129–132, 199–202). Emma was deeply unhappy during this period and considered herself to be living in a menage a trois.

Nevertheless, she persevered, trying to hold onto the belief that her insecure husband needed her and would not forsake the marriage because he needed her calming demeanour and her innate sense of grandeur. Such characteristics in a spouse were crucial in preventing Carl from lapsing into insanity at times.

The synopsis evidences Carl's attachment difficulties and his struggle to remain attached to one constant figure. These facts provide us with evidence that Carl suffered severely from attachment difficulties throughout his life.

Period of Traumatic Experience

I am sure it is clear from the foregoing description that Carl Jung's major experience of trauma constituted his frequent separations from his mother whilst he was growing up. In addition, his mother's location during these times was never discussed; nor were reasons given for her absences, which in actuality remained clouded in mystery, sometimes being thought to be a consequence of mental illness, at other times believed to be a result of marital difficulties. Carl did recall that when his mother returned home, he would hear strange noises emanating from her bedroom and believed he saw monsters and headless creatures coming out from her bedroom (Jung and Jaffe, 2019, p. 32). It seems to me that he was describing the trials of a child who has witnessed traumatic episodes of a parent's schizophrenic illness. He later described his feelings of not being able to breathe and of choking as being "psychogenic" in origin.

As if this had not proved sufficient trauma for one person to endure, the young adult Carl was then presented with the task of nursing his father through a terminal illness and losing, during early adulthood, the one parent who gave him some sense of security.

Evidence of Periods of Mental Disturbance

At age twelve, the young Carl suffered a period when his parents feared that their son was epileptic. This is still seen as a serious affliction for anyone but all the more so when it occurred within a poor family who had no resources to support a son throughout his adult life. A fellow schoolboy had pushed Carl over in the *Munsterplatz*, and Carl had hit his head on a kerbstone. As a consequence, he was only partially conscious for a while. He remembered thinking that this would mean he did not have to attend the Gymnasium. In fact, he then suffered repeated fainting fits and consequently missed school for six months (ibid, pp. 47–49). Although Carl was known as a very able pupil, he found the social aspects of school particularly difficult and very much preferred his own company at home. However, when he overheard his parents expressing anxiety about his health and his future ability to earn a living, he decided that the fainting fits had to stop. He went back to school, only fainting once more. He also began to study in earnest, rising sometimes at three in the morning to study before the long walk to school. He said that it was at this point that he learned the nature of a neurosis (ibid, p. 49).

When Emma refused his first marriage proposal, the young adult Carl effectively suffered a mental breakdown. The experience of loss proved on a number of occasions to lead him to suffer periods of breakdown. Again, he suffered another significant loss when he ceased (what he termed) his "religious crush" on Sigmund Freud (Freud/Jung Letters, McGuire, 1974, p. 131). Carl went on to suffer a breakdown which persisted for a number of years, during which he disappeared from public view, becoming a virtual recluse. It is thought that Carl never fully recovered from the schism with Freud. Despite the fact that Freud wanted Jung to be "his son and heir" (Bair, 2004, p. 115), the cracks in their relationship were visible from early in their friendship; Carl could not agree with Freud's belief that the cause of all neuroses lay in difficulties with sexuality (Jung and Jaffe, 2019, p. 179; Dunne, 2015, pp. 61–64). Freud had begun by theorising that all neuroses were a result of a young person's experience of sexual abuse, often by a family member. As I have written before (Fear, 2016), I suggest that this view scandalised the strict propriety of upper-class Viennese society, and had Freud persisted with this belief, it would have led to the withdrawal of the 'troubled' rich daughters from treatment by Freud. Consequently, it is my belief that Freud amended his theory to espouse that neurosis is the consequence of the patient's inner sexual fantasies. Either way, the young adult Carl could not agree with Freud, probably because this seduction theory may have indicated that the cause of his own neurosis was rooted in his own very real experience of sexual abuse. As a young person, he had been abused by a man whom he worshipped at the time. He admitted the details to Freud during the work he undertook with Freud on repressed memories in October 1907. Carl's son, Franz, described how his father was mentally very disturbed after his schism with Freud, stating that his father suffered a period of semi-madness. He told of how his father would lock himself away in his *Kabinett* (office) and sleep with a gun by his bed in case he could no longer bear the suffering (Clay, 2016, p. 227).

Again, a further period of loss brought another breakdown. When Emma died in 1955, Carl Jung became a virtual recluse and busied himself at Bollingen, where he had built three towers (along the lake from Kusnacht, their marital home, on the shores of Lake Lucerne) (Dunne, 2015, pp. 134–138; Jung and Jaffe, 2019, pp. 267, 269–270). Carl lived at Bollingen a hermit-like existence; the living accommodation of the main tower was circular, composed of a room with a central hearth; no windows; a central sitting area around the hearth with bunks around the circumference of the room. There was no water or electricity or central heating as the family enjoyed at their main home on the lakeside. Carl had become obsessed with the building of towers because they reminded him of his monumental phallus dream when he was a child (Jung and Jaffe, 2019, pp. 25–26).

As a direct result of Carl's series of affairs, Emma threatened divorce three times when she could no longer contain her anguish and humiliation (Bair, 2004, p. 157). Each threat was followed by a period of mental instability in Carl, during which he would relinquish his patients to the care of Emma (who had herself trained as an analyst in her thirties). Carl would suffer periods of intense gastric upset and bouts of influenza which confined him to bed, just as he had suffered as a child. Emma grew accustomed to this behaviour, abandoning her decision to divorce him because she felt it was her wifely duty to help him recover from the illnesses. Gradually, she became convinced that Carl would never leave her because of the stability that she provided with her enduring love.

Carl admitted his mental instability in a letter to Sabina Spielrein (Clay, 2016, p. 161; *Carotenuto*, 1982, p. 93) during the years that he was close to her. When he was writing his second book, he professed that he heard voices dictating to him (Clay, 2016, p. 218). From this point on, he lost the scientific objectivity that he had acquired during his medical training and was overtaken by his obsession with the occult.

Carl's Quest in Life

Whilst working in the Army Medical Corps, living without Emma at the Chateau D'Oex (where a frequent visitor was Toni Wolff) he suffered a schizophrenic episode. This was sometimes referred to as 'his creative illness' by colleagues who believed that it enabled him to make sense of symbolisation and unconscious processes. Writing and studying unconscious processes and spiritualistic events represented Carl's quest in life. His wife was also driven by a quest – she was researching and writing her book on the knight Perceval, whose own quest for the Holy Grail became her personal quest. This work, which had fascinated Emma since her early teens, took Emma so much time and research that she died before finishing the book. It was Carl who actually finished and arranged for the publication of her life's work.

Was Carl 'Different From the Norm'?

It seems to me that this chapter has revealed that here we see a very troubled man, who undoubtedly was plagued from his early years with psychological disturbance. It is tragic that he lost his father in very early adulthood, but the effect of this loss was undoubtedly exacerbated by his mother's psychic disturbance and frequent absences, which would have been difficult for Carl to comprehend.

Gret, his second daughter, stated that no normal man would love a woman like Toni Wolff. Indeed, photographs of her display a very hard-faced, unsmiling, unattractive and unbending woman who lacked any attribute of femininity. However, she fascinated the adult Carl, who spent long hours closeted with her in the privacy of his *Kabinett* or at his self-constructed 'fantasy' tower dwelling at Bollingen. When Toni died suddenly in her sleep in 1953, aged sixty-five, he could not trust himself to attend her funeral for fear that he would not be able to contain his emotions. His wife attended, and although Toni's presence must have been tortuous for her for quite some years, she sagely remarked that she was grateful to Toni Wolff, who was able to provide what Carl needed at a very difficult time in his life – something that even she was not able to do. She felt that he had needed both his wife and Toni in his life in order to cope with Personality Number One and Personality Number Two.

Carl's World View

It was difficult at first for the researcher to know which of the four world views – Romantic, Comic, Ironic and Tragic – to attribute to Carl Jung. The way in which Carl Jung approached his quest to build a house for himself and his family at Kusnacht on the banks of the lake seemed to me to be a Romantic notion. It followed a childhood obsession that he must live near water after a visit with his mother to Lake Constance (Jung and Jaffe, 2019, p. 20). He then redoubled his obsession with water and loyalty to his peasant beginnings by building a second house in a medieval style with several giant towers – all of which involved huge excesses in terms of both architecture and expense. Consequently, I think that his *weltanschauung* contained elements of the Romantic world view. The initial plans for both of the houses, which he himself drew up, reflect that he believed that anything was possible – akin to the humanistic concept of self-actualisation. Undoubtedly, he lived a life influenced by the occult – hearing voices, seeing heads without bodies floating past, believing absolutely in the world of spirits. He told no one, throughout his life, of his dream of the phallic, one-eyed creature in a huge stone hallway, of his preoccupation with his manikin nor of his wonderings about the stone. Yet these visions repeatedly troubled and preoccupied him throughout his life. He lived in a secret inner world of introspection.

Despite these Romantic elements, it seems true to say that for much of his life, Carl was profoundly troubled and unhappy; most definitely this indicates a person adhering to a Tragic world view. Maybe he thought that if he could live in a polygamous society, then some of his dissatisfaction would evaporate. His determination to flaunt his 'other women' indicates that he envisaged himself as omnipotent and that he harboured grandiose fantasies. He seems to have been unaffected by the censure that such behaviour brought with it. He also felt that had he been able to be the patriarch who alone provided his family with financial security, he would have been happier (Bair, 2004, p. 114). Emma's own fortune, though useful, made this impossible to achieve. The fact that he was absorbed in his own misery for much of his life points to a Tragic world view rather than to the less pessimistic Ironic vision of reality. He very much felt that the past affects the present, and it cannot be undone or forgotten. As the Tragic vision states, not all is redeemable and not all can be remedied. He wisely stated early in his career at the Burgholzli, that one had to learn the story of an individual's life if one was to be able to find the source of his or her mental disturbance. He disliked the fact that psychiatrists were only interested in diagnosis of mental illness but did not work to cure individuals (ibid, pp. 141–144); in those days, such mental illness just led to incarceration. It is the truth, though, that in Jung's day, there were none of the drugs that today's psychiatrists can at least prescribe.

Conclusion

It seems likely that the reader will agree that Carl was undoubtedly a troubled soul. He was also highly individualistic. His life story is incredible, but many people would find his omnipotence and arrogance displeasing and unappealing. It is as if he was stuck in a certain very uncomfortable groove from which he could not escape; namely, the occult. In summary, I feel that overall, he held a Tragic world view. This is not surprising given the early trauma in his life and his lifelong struggle to achieve that sense of 'merging' that he had once experienced with his father.

Chapter 10

The Life of John Bowlby

Introduction

Edward John Mostyn Bowlby was one of six children, born to his mother, May Mostyn, and his father, Major-General Sir Anthony Bowlby (1855–1929). He was born on February 26, 1907 when his parents were middle-aged; his mother being forty and his father fifty-two. With two elder sisters and a brother, Tony, who was thirteen months his senior, he was the fourth of their six children. His mother was quite disinterested in her children; she also made it apparent that Tony was her undeniable favourite. Maybe as a consequence of this, John and Tony developed an extremely rivalrous and competitive relationship, perhaps exacerbated by the fact that the two boys were often mistaken as twins. A third younger brother suffered from learning difficulties, and the family found it hard to come to terms with the idea that this child was not destined for success in the way typically anticipated in their family. John's experience of growing up alongside a child with 'differences' may well account for the fact that he felt attuned to children who suffered from disadvantage.

A Sub-Optimal Attachment Schema With Disdain for Authority

I would like to thank Jeremy Holmes (1993) for his excellent biography of John Bowlby, which I have used a great deal in assessment of Bowlby's attachment schema.

As was typical in the first half of the twentieth century in the life of an upper-middle-class family, John and his siblings were left to the daily care of their nanny. She had joined the family when the first child was born and remained with the family until she was in her nineties. He did not see much of his mother; she visited the nursery every morning after breakfast, and the children were taken to be with her from 5.00 until 6.00 each evening. She often spent this time reading to them, particularly from a favourite book of hers: *Children of the New Forest*. I guess she was enthralled with the New Forest, because she took the children there every July for a vacation. The family also spent time together for six weeks in late July

DOI: 10.4324/9781003316503-11

and August, when they would habitually visit the Scottish Highlands. In consequence, we might say that his mother was intermittently physically present, but it is questionable whether she was emotionally available apart from her determination to teach the children about the joys of the countryside. Perhaps this is the reason that Bowlby argued pertinently in attachment theory that it is not a question of how much time a child spends with a mother or 'mother-substitute' – it is more the question of the *quality* of the relationship with a parental figure. Whilst John's nanny remained a constant figure, in reality, the day-to-day care of each of the children was left to a nursemaid. John was deeply attached to a nursemaid called Minnie, and it proved very disturbing for him when she (as a 'mother-substitute') left the family when he was just four years of age.

When the First World War broke out in 1914, their parents made the danger of bombing the rationale for despatching their children to boarding school. With a noticeably acerbic manner, John commented that this was a thinly veiled attempt to cover the reality that it was normal procedure in order that the schools could cultivate the phlegm that characterised an English gentleman. John clearly found his upbringing unsatisfactory; it was the reason that he suffered from a distinct disadvantage that he endured throughout his life: namely, the struggle to be intimate with family and friends. Even though he decided that his own family should live for a time *en famille* with the Sutherlands in Hampstead, Jock Sutherland (Sutherland, 1991) was known to remark on Bowlby's aloof and somewhat distant, formal manner.

When John first left school, he began a career in the Royal Navy at Dartmouth College. Despite showing distinct signs of success, he disliked the repressive attitude within Navy circles and its authoritarian regime and so requested that his father buy him out. We see here a first instance in adulthood of John's abiding dislike and disdain for authority and narrow-mindedness. This somewhat arrogant disdain for authority and refusal to submit to the cohesiveness that is thought to come with adherence to 'the rules' was seen time and again in Bowlby. We can detect it later in John's life by his attitude towards the propriety of the British Psycho-Analytical Society. Whilst in training as an analyst, he was said to have argued with both his training analyst, Joan Riviere, and his supervisor, Melanie Klein. Once qualified in 1937, he presented his ground-breaking paper, *Forty-Four Juvenile Thieves: Their Characters and Home Life* (Bowlby, 1944). From his time as an analysand onwards, Bowlby was known to frequently dissent from the received wisdom of the day, refusing to give precedence to those in authority. He felt strongly that psychoanalysis had become underpinned by philosophy and hermeneutics and should return to employing the rigours of science. Throughout his life, he charted a course that evidenced that he set out, consciously, to differ from the norm. Again, we can recognise this theme that wounded healers 'differed from the norm'. This characteristic is frequently marked by a disdain for authority.

John left the Navy and went up to Trinity College, Cambridge, in order to read pre-clinical sciences and psychology. No doubt his father was partly agreeable to this because he was happy that his second son was showing a determination to follow in his footsteps. Major-General Sir Anthony Bowlby was an eminent surgeon, appointed as Royal Surgeon to both King Edward VII and King George V. He worked long hours at a career with which he was obsessed, and so the children rarely spent time with him apart from the family's long summer vacations in Scotland. Tony, the eldest son, had been encouraged to follow in his father's footsteps, but possibly because he feared the prospect of being deemed a relative failure in comparison to his father's prowess, he chose to follow a different path. This left the path of medicine open to John, and it is surmised that he may have taken this step believing it would please his father.

Directly after John Bowlby achieved a First-Class Honours degree from Cambridge, his rebellious streak showed itself once again. Rather than go to London to study clinical medicine as was anticipated, Bowlby found employment in a school for maladjusted children. This move proved to be decisive in terms of his whole career – two occurrences steered the course from then on. Firstly, he found that he had a talent for relating to the boys who were encountering difficulties; he found himself capable of experiencing a deep empathic understanding of them. This was no doubt a function of his own difficult attachment history; his feeling that he had not enjoyed a close relationship with his parents or siblings combined with his experience of living alongside a younger brother with learning difficulties. One boy at the school, who had been thrown out of public school for repeated episodes of stealing, followed him about wherever he went. John was able to make the link between difficult attachment history and repeated episodes of delinquency. Working with these boys was to change the course of his life's work. His meeting with John Alford was to be a second seminal chance event. Alford had enjoyed a period in personal therapy himself and found it useful; it was he who suggested that Bowlby train as an analyst.

Bowlby took Alford up on his suggestion and was accepted by the Institute of Psychoanalysis to train as an analyst. At the same time, he continued with his clinical training in London in order to qualify as a doctor. He qualified as an analyst in 1937, by which time he was working at the Child Guidance Clinic. In order to achieve full voting rights within the Institute, the individual had to present a paper. Bowlby presented a paper that was published in 1940 in *The International Journal of Psycho-Analysis*: 'The Influence of the Environment in the Development of the Neuroses and Neurotic Character'. The paper was commented upon as being "Very interesting. But what has this to do with psychoanalysis?" (Holmes, 1993). It seems to me that this comment encapsulates the problem that Bowlby was to encounter repeatedly throughout his career. Even in the current climate of opinion in the second decade of the twenty-first century, my own book on attachment theory has encountered a similar reaction in some spheres. A debate continues to rage about the cause of neurosis. Which is more important as the cause of neurosis: intrapsychic conflict or environmental factors? I find it hard to accept that most individuals of a psychoanalytic persuasion feel that the two are mutually exclusive. Is it not possible for there to exist a continuum and for us all to place ourselves somewhere on that continuum?

Bowlby followed this first presentation in the Institute with a second seminal paper in 1944, also based upon his work at the Child Guidance Clinic. This paper, entitled *Forty-Four Juvenile Thieves: Their Characters and Home Life* (Bowlby, 1944), was to bring him to the notice of government.

During the Second World War, Bowlby served as an army psychiatrist and psychotherapist and was part of what was known as the 'invisible college': a group of men who were relied upon to review the efficacy of officer selection. In 1944, the president of the Psycho-Analytic Society, Sylvia Payne (herself an Independent) proposed Bowlby for the position of Training Secretary. Despite not having been appointed a training analyst, Bowlby was duly elected, probably as a consequence of his organisational skills, sense of balance and authoritative demeanour.

Towards the end of his time in analysis, John began to feel the need to settle down, and in 1937, he met the seven sisters of a pipe-smoking Mrs Longstaff whilst on holiday in the New Forest. He became enchanted with the third daughter (Ursula), who was both intelligent and beautiful. Within a year, the couple were married. John and Ursula had four children, but John largely left the care of their children in his wife's hands. He was regarded as a remote and 'not very present' father. One of his sons is said to have remarked that he wondered whether his father was a burglar, because he rarely came home until after dark and never talked about his work! As so often happens with psychopathology, John repeated the pattern set by his own father: he believed in hard work but, like his father, was determined to take his family on long holidays to Scotland (buying a property on his beloved Isle of Skye) in order to teach them to appreciate the natural world. His daughter Mary commented that her father was a dedicated and "fun" grandfather, giving to his grandchildren the time, tolerance and amusing attitude that he lacked in his years as a parent. Perhaps this was again a learned process: John had always had fun with his loving grandfather, 'Grampy' (his maternal grandfather). I wonder if, in fact, his appreciation of how a secure attachment relationship feels comes from his own experience with Grampy and with the nursemaid, Minnie. It would seem that John knew at an intellectual level all too well the effects of dysfunctional parenting, which in fact he abhorred. I think this is the underlying reason that he campaigned so hard all his adult life for the pre-eminent need for the child to experience a good attachment relationship. He comments about the dangers of suppressing feelings: he talks about the way in which in some families, the child's dependency needs are regarded as something to be grown out of as quickly as possible, and the crying child is greeted without any form of empathic attunement (Bowlby, 1979).

Drive for Sense of Connection

Bowlby believed passionately that a person is only able to actively display his or her own feelings in front of friends and relatives if they have enjoyed an acceptance of their feelings by their principal attachment objects during childhood.

Bowlby himself realised that he was deficient in this respect as a result of his exposure to the 'stiff upper lip' (phlegm) taught at boarding school. This is an integral feature of what he termed 'the making of an English gentleman', and in fact, he abhorred this way of bringing up children. It may well be that he considered his upbringing – born into a family that had consciously taken the decision to avoid the processing of emotion, where parents were distant (both physically and emotionally) and did not advocate the sharing of confidences and feelings – to have meant that he and his siblings suffered a form of emotional abuse. In being able to accurately recognise this, he found that it came easily to empathise with the children from disadvantaged families, about which he coined the evocative phrase "affectionless psychopaths". He was, of course, referring to the way in which the teenagers he met in the Child Guidance Clinic had lost contact, either for a prolonged period of time or permanently, with their attachment objects. He noted that such individuals were wont to play out their frustrations and dissatisfaction with society – what sociologists call 'alienation' and 'anomie' – by repeatedly displaying delinquent behaviour within the society in which they live.

Bowlby was acutely aware of his own difficulties regarding intimate relationships – as seen in the sense of distance from his own children and from his friends. John Bowlby recognised that we all have an intuitive need to stay in close proximity to our attachment figures. No doubt this is the reason that Mary Ainsworth declared that the centrality of the purpose of attachment-seeking behaviour became obvious to Bowlby when he heard about Konrad Lorenz's study of the behaviour of greylag goslings (Lorenz, 1937). Lorenz discovered that goslings are prone, for a discrete period of their youth, to (what he termed) 'imprinting'. This occurs when the gosling seeks to remain close to any moving object that it has espied during this stage. Lorenz even proved that a gosling would attach itself – incredibly – to a human being (such as himself) or to a moving cardboard box during this life stage.

Despite John Bowlby's difficulties with intimate human relationships, he devoted his entire adult life to the study of the effect of difficult attachment experiences on the growing child. He put forward the theory that it is environmental influence that causes neurosis rather than intrapsychic conflict, this latter belief having been widely ignored by those of the Freudian and Kleinian schools. It is this seminal difference in belief system that led to Bowlby being ostracised by the majority in the Institute of Psycho-Analysis. As a consequence, he had little contact with the institute after the 1960s. His recognition of the traumatic effects of insecure attachment experiences led to his spending a great deal of his time researching and lecturing on the effects of maternal deprivation. We could say that the term 'maternal deprivation' is something of a misnomer – as I have said elsewhere (Fear, 2016). It is true that many disadvantaged individuals do not suffer so much from maternal deprivation (i.e. the removal of a secure base that they have enjoyed for some time in their childhoods) as 'privation' (i.e. they have never known what it feels like to feel secure).

The Nature of Bowlby's Quest in Life

Thus, I believe, we can readily perceive that John Bowlby's quest in life concerned his determination to modify Western perceptions so that more individuals experience secure attachment within their families during childhood. His work did, of course, lead to huge changes within childcare. The change first came into being as a result of his co-operation with James Robertson in making a film entitled *A Two-Year-Old Goes to Hospital* (Bowlby and Robertson, 1952a). This is a film about a two-year-old who is left in hospital by her parents and who obviously experiences the stages of 'Protest, Despair and Detachment' (as defined by Bowlby and Robertson); it is a film that is difficult to watch without tears in your eyes. The child is fortunate if her/his parents are able to visit for an hour twice a week. I suffered an almost identical experience, feeling 'abandoned' in Harrogate General Hospital for twenty-six days at the age of three, almost concurrently with the making of this film. I remember all too vividly being scolded by the nurses for crying because I was missing my mummy and being entrusted with the care of a one-year-old infant who was placed on my bed, with the cot sides of the bed raised, so that I could amuse him! I was fortunate (or unfortunate!) enough to be allowed parental visiting three times during my twenty-six-day stay in hospital! Bowlby and Robertson's film (1952a) led to seminal changes in the way that parents are now encouraged to have unimpeded access to their children whilst in hospital.

This is certainly one area that Bowlby achieved real change as a result of his quest in life. We have also witnessed great changes as a direct result of his work in the field of social care of children. Bowlby was commissioned to write a report for the World Health Organization (WHO) shortly after the end of the Second World War on the subject of homeless children. As a direct result, we have witnessed a sea change regarding the taking of children into care. Nowadays, social workers are taught to avoid the removal of children from their parents if at all possible. Changes have also been apparent in the vetting system for those children seeking adoptive parents and in the running of children's homes for those who have no parent able to take daily care of them.

Weltanschauung: World View

John Bowlby's dominant world view was inescapably Ironic. Certainly, he was fascinated by the vicissitudes of life – thus, he gave much of his thought and time to the negatives experienced by many. I interpret that this fascination with the negatives stems from his own experience in childhood. The reality of his upbringing represents a strange paradox – in many aspects, he was fortunate enough to have been born into an upper-class, wealthy family of some renown. Both his father and grandfather had enjoyed favours from royalty as a result of their prowess as medical men. His grandfather had been a part of the Raj in India in the days of the British Empire. However, the family experienced tragedy when his grand-father was murdered in India, and in consequence, John's father had decided that he should take on the task of taking care of his widowed mother until her demise. It was only then that he felt free enough of constraints to be able to look for a wife with whom to make a family life of his own. Consequently, he married rather late in life. John had a privileged upbringing, but an integral part of that meant that he spent a large proportion of his youth in the impersonal, emotion-free setting of an English public school. We are reminded here, in John's life, of Neville Syming-ton's and Patrick Casement's life stories, the price that was extorted for 'enjoying' such a privilege. In John Bowlby's life story, we can clearly observe the way in which, having been taught to repress one's emotions and to cope with the vicis-situdes of life stoically, John was consequently unable to find a way in which he could communicate easily and meaningfully with his own children. Perhaps it is significant that I cannot find comments upon his marital relationship in any biog-raphy. Undeniably, it is true that he and his wife remained married. Domestically, there was a clear division of labour – John worked extremely hard in his role as breadwinner, although I surmise that his devotion to his work also stemmed from the sense of satisfaction derived thereby. His wife was responsible for running the household, giving birth to, and raising the children.

Once having qualified in pre-clinical sciences at Cambridge, John was drawn towards the tribulations of life and their effects upon the security of the individual. As I have commented upon earlier, instead of completing his medical training, Bowlby chose to work at a school for maladjusted children. Clearly, he found satisfaction in his capacity to communicate with and understand the world of these troubled young people. This experience was to set a course for his journey through life; even whilst involved in his clinical training, John embarked upon a training in psychoanalysis and upon introspection and an interest in the challeng-ing effects of a dysfunctional environment upon the individual. Consequent upon this time in his early career, Bowlby wrote his famous paper on the forty-four juvenile thieves – his "affectionless psychopaths". There followed a period of work in the Child Guidance Clinic, working with children and their mothers to undo the effects of a dysfunctional environment. However, he worked assiduously to find ways in which to undo those negative environmental impacts. Ever a focus on the negatives! Thus, his world view evidences no likeness to the Romantic or Comic visions of reality. Together with Mary Ainsworth, he put forward a theory about attachment (Bowlby, 1979, 1988), which may at times seem banal and have a tinge of the obvious, but nevertheless, we should not forget that despite this, no-one else had previously stuck their head above the parapet – promptly to have it decapitated by the leading psychoanalysts! Even the normally fair-minded Don-ald Winnicott, who himself admitted that Bowlby had always responded to his own papers positively, expressed an irritation in response to Bowlby's papers and publications!

Again, in being commissioned by the WHO to research a paper on the effect of homeless children living in institutional settings, John Bowlby once again demonstrated his proclivity to focus upon the negatives. He spent his time investigating the effects upon those individuals who he believed had drawn a short straw in life.

However, whether we are focussing upon his juvenile thieves, the children incarcerated in hospital or the lives of those in orphanages, Bowlby sought consistently to work towards change for the better. This is a clear illustration of his Ironic *weltanschauung*. He too managed to turn a negative into a positive. He turned the metaphorical coin over and spent time studying the other side in order to find a positive solution.

As I have already stated, he found his role as a parent difficult, but we hear that by the time he became a grandparent, he had modified his behaviour so that he was able to join his grandchildren in fascinating play and fun. With his own children, it seems unequivocal that he found intimacy difficult, but nevertheless, he obviously cared for his family ceaselessly, making sure (just like his mother) that they developed an appreciation of the natural world. He derived a deep sense of satisfaction from this. I suggest that it is not mere chance that he died at his home in the Isle of Skye and had instructed that he was given a traditional, simple Skye funeral, involving three 'lifts' of the coffin from the home to his resting place.

John Bowlby may not have found intimate relationships easy at an experiential level, but undeniably, he used his awareness of his difficulties resulting from less-than-ideal attachment practices to inform millions of us how best we can avoid providing our children with experiences of family life from which they would be forced to suffer the lifetime legacy of an insecure attachment schema.

Conclusion

We all owe John Bowlby a debt of gratitude for his seminal work on attachment theory. As a consequence of his work, we all may have been touched by the changes in social policy and the way we care for our children. I have no doubt that his world view was Ironic, for he searched for and found a way to turn the negatives into positives. Certainly, he suffered from a sub-optimal attachment experience, and I would suggest that his time in boarding school may well have been experienced as a trauma by John. However, these experiences served to enable him to develop the quest in life for which he is well renowned. Like other subjects of my research, John Bowlby's behaviour evidenced a disregard and disdain for authority, and in this way, he 'differed from the norm'.

Chapter 11

Analysis of Themes in the Research

Introduction

In this chapter, I intend to draw together the six themes that you will have seen emerge from the analysis of the data. Whilst these are named 'categories' by Glaser and Strauss, I have chosen to call them 'themes' in this book.

The Experience of Trauma in the Individual's Life

I have used the life stories of seven psychotherapists and psychoanalysts as the source of the data in this research. It appeared that each individual suffered from at least one difficult, personally traumatic period during their early lives. I use the term 'early lives' to encompass childhood, adolescence or early adulthood.

For some, such as Nina Coltart, the trauma primarily derived from a single devastating occurrence, whilst for others, such as Neville Symington and Patrick Casement, the difficulty permeated the whole of their early lives, including a period of psychic conflict for each during early adulthood. Carl Jung similarly endured a childhood beset with insecurity because of his mother's frequent absences as a result of her own mental instability and her unhappy marriage to Carl's father. This instability was increased when Carl's father died shortly before he had even graduated from university. Any significant loss thereafter for Carl was followed by a period of breakdown. Franz, Carl's son, felt that his father never recovered fully from his schism with Freud. After his wife died, Carl became a virtual recluse, living at his tower dwelling at Bollingen.

However, even when one begins to analyse a single traumatic incident, it is often possible to identify antecedents that have indeed coloured that event, making it in actuality considerably more traumatic than it would otherwise have been. Perhaps it would be more accurate to state that, often, a single event is important because it represents a sort of catalyst – 'the last straw' which makes the underlying difficulty come to full conscious awareness. Nina Coltart's life provides a case in point – she stated that her personal attachment difficulties emanating from the sudden loss of both parents (who died in a train crash) had, in actuality, an antecedent: she had suffered numerous small losses because her nanny (her

DOI: 10.4324/9781003316503-12

primary love object) frequently went missing when she was called away to nurse new mothers in the village, but Nina did not know where she had gone or if she would return.

For others, however, such as Viktor Frankl, early years seemed to be unremarkable, but the events which followed during his early adulthood drew attention to the difficulties in his upbringing – the constant severe discrimination against his ethnicity as a member of the Jewish fraternity during the early 1930s as Hitler gradually gained complete power in Germany. He remembers how he was walking with his father when a man tipped his father's hat from his head into the gutter. He remembers asking his father what the meaning of this was and being told it was an integral part of the discrimination against Jews and should be borne stoically and without comment.

It is surely true to say that for many of us, our growing-up years are punctuated by difficult events or circumstances. However, the same event was not necessarily experienced in the same way by different individuals. For instance, Patrick Casement and Neville Symington both attended boarding school. Whilst Neville Symington angrily names Ampleforth College, his boarding school, "Yorkshire's concentration camp", Patrick Casement felt that his parents' decision to send him to boarding school was one of the best decisions they ever made. He felt that the physical presence of boarding schools provided a constancy that his parents' peripatetic lives lacked. With regard to both analysts, their education at boarding school appears at first glance to be the feature that draws one's attention, but one gradually deduces, by careful analysis, that difficulties existed within the family of origin and that the resulting complications led to the parental decision to send the child (or children) to boarding school. Patrick Casement admits that his sense of security derived from places rather than people, who kept leaving him, so in consequence he became comforted by the constancy of these institutions: his little church at Terwick, his prep school at Maidwell, Winchester College and Winchester Cathedral, where he sang in the choir during a summer spent at school.

Thus, I feel that one needs to study the whole picture of a person's life in order to appreciate the reason that a single event proves to be such a defining moment in their life. Indeed, Jung stated that to understand an individual's mental disturbance, one needs to look at his or her early life in order to fully understand that person's difficulties. I am sure, that if you are a psychoanalytic therapist, you will be well versed in carrying out such a complex process of analysis. This needs to be completed for one to discover the full implications beneath a patient's presenting problem. However, for those of us who are not so familiar with the therapy world or work within the cognitive behavioural modality, there is a tendency to look at the consciously held belief systems of a person and to note their cognitive dissonance rather than to give prominence to the factors that underlie any traumatic event.

I have come to understand that one precise trauma is not necessarily of prime importance – it is rather the compelling realisation that the individual has suffered from significant internal conflict during early years of their life. I draw your attention to the early life of Carl Jung, Patrick Casement, Neville Symington, Nina Coltart, Viktor Frankl, John Bowlby and Sigmund Freud. I am promulgating the notion that in actuality, each individual has undergone a time of considerable and often prolonged suffering and that it is such personal suffering that enables the budding therapist to empathise with the pain of others. The pain suffered enables the therapist to be able to create a sense of 'connection' with their patients when the latter present in the consulting room. Stern (1985) referred to this quality in a mother–child relationship as "attunement". In short, woundedness fuels the countertransference of the therapist. In my earlier writings on attachment theory (Fear, 2017), I put forward an integrative theory which is underpinned by the concept of learned security, which involves the process of "intersubjective empathy" (ibid, pp. 146, 233). Intersubjective empathy requires that the therapist is not only capable of standing in that other person's shoes but is also ready, willing and able to engage in a process of *checking out her understanding* of *the feelings involved* by engaging with the patient in a constant process of clarification, a process of mutual collaboration in making a joined-up narrative of the patient's life. It is my belief that the therapist is more able to carry out such a process if she has herself suffered considerably in her early years. It is not purely that she has suffered but that she has developed a degree of compulsive fascination with the concept of suffering. In consequence, she finds herself drawn to individuals who have suffered as well and is unconsciously (or sometimes consciously) compelled to provide 'the other' with some form of succour. Essentially, I think we can say that the therapist has gone through a process of 'sensitisation' to the wounds of others.

My research indicates that the presence of early trauma in an individual's life is connected, very often, with the second theme that I will now proceed to discuss. I have briefly alluded to it in the preceding paragraph. It is the drive for a sense of connection. My research enables me to put forward the thesis that the presence of early trauma and this second theme – that of attachment difficulties – are frequently entwined.

Attachment Difficulties: The Drive for a Sense of 'Connection'

As a consequence of the individual's early history, I found that I repeatedly deduced that the subject suffered from a sub-optimal attachment schema. As stated in an earlier chapter, it is a little-known statistic yet an accurate truth that only two-thirds of the population in Western Europe (Van Ijzendoorn and Kroonenberg, 1988) are fortunate enough to experience an upbringing from which they develop a secure attachment schema.

My analysis tells me that each individual whose life I have studied possesses a sub-optimal attachment schema: either an insecure ambivalent or insecure avoidant attachment. A person with an insecure ambivalent attachment schema will tend to experience a constant conflict and a tension in their feelings as a result of experiencing both negative and positive emotions in respect of the attachment object (usually but not necessarily a parent; Neville Symington was much attached to the household's maids). This means that, in effect, the person is deeply attached to a single individual and that for some of the time, he may have a tendency to be needy and uncertain or anxious about whether his object will reciprocate his love and, indeed, provide succour to his neediness. At other times, the individual with an insecure ambivalent attachment schema will display some hostility towards his attachment figure, finding himself to be suffused with rage, anger, irritation, jealousy and perhaps a desire for retribution, all of which are negative emotions, as opposed to the positive feelings of love, admiration, reliance. (Hence the term 'ambivalent'.) Carl Jung's marital relationship with his wife, Emma, undoubtedly evidenced this ambivalence. He loved her deeply and needed her calm demeanour, yet his numerous affairs were surely an acting out of the anger that he was feeling against Emma – perhaps a feeling emanating from a resentment about just how much he needed her and anger about her independent wealth and her capacity to remain calm.

Alternatively, other individuals whose lives I have studied tend towards what is known as an insecure avoidant attachment schema. This schema usually develops psychologically after an individual has suffered an overwhelming experience of deeply painful rejection or loss in early years. As a consequence of this, she has 'decided' (usually unconsciously) to never again risk the vulnerability which ensues when one dares to involve oneself in a full attachment to another living soul. This means, in consequence, that she is loath to make any really intimate relationships, and tends to steer clear of becoming involved in any relationship other than at a superficial level. As a consequence of this, she suffers from a feeling of 'disconnect' – which is frequently accompanied by a belief that life lacks meaning. This is often felt as a result of persistent avoidance of meaningful relationships and is accompanied by a pervasive sense of existential dissatisfaction. Unconsciously, if the person is an analyst, she may then seek to find some satisfaction through the making of an intimate environment in the consulting room. Such relationships, whilst highly satisfying, do not necessitate a compromise of her vulnerability, because therapeutic relationships are not mutually reciprocal. Frequently, as time goes by, she may dare to invest emotionally in some other individual in her personal life, but by that juncture, her career choice to train as a therapist has been taken. Again, I stress that the reason for her career decision is often unconscious, because her defensive structure is not conscious.

Nina Coltart's life story provides the most obvious example of this process. Having endured the pain and rage of losing both of her parents suddenly, she consciously decided not to have a partner or children, for she was so scared that she might leave them. She maintained ties to individuals with whom she corresponded but did not encourage any meetings. She describes her favourite evening as having been warmly invited to a party next door, and though she can hear the chatter and noise, she prefers to stay at home and read a book. I think this pronouncement encapsulates my idea that someone with an insecure avoidant schema avoids true intimacy at all costs. Similarly, a friend's suggestion that they meet for the first time in London led Nina to refuse this request, saying that it might spoil the relationship.

The therapeutic relationships in which therapists become involved tend to satisfy a desire for what I term 'connection'. However, I think it is worth noting that this sense of connection is somewhat one-sided – to which I alluded earlier. In the therapy relationship, the patient (client, analysand) shares his innermost secrets, dreads and fears, but this is not reciprocated by the therapist, who does not talk about her own vulnerabilities. The point that I am making is that the relationship is, perforce, unbalanced; it lacks mutual reciprocity. Correctly, it is the function of the therapist to provide a "containing" relationship (Bion, 1970, 1984). This can only be achieved by the therapist following the 'rule of abstinence'. It is correctly deemed unethical for the therapist to use the relationship to process her own inner dreads, fears, problems. In consequence, the relationship is skewed, necessarily, towards the provision of an intimate environment *by the therapist* for the satisfaction of the patient. In addition, the unbalanced nature of the transference–countertransference relationship is an additional reason for the lack of mutual reciprocity. It is true that as therapists, we are rewarded by a feeling of intimacy and 'connection' – but the point that I am making is that it is derived from an unequal relationship in which the therapist takes care not to render herself vulnerable. This is not to deny that the therapeutic relationships in which we involve ourselves do not cost us dearly at times, and I am sure that you can all testify to times in which you have sought succour from your own supervisor or therapist as a result of the counter-transference that arises in response to your patient. You may well have suffered a sleepless night on occasion!

In consequence of the asymmetry of the relationship, the therapist is thus able to achieve a sense of connection without also experiencing a growing vulnerability on one's own part as the therapeutic relationship grows in meaning. The therapeutic relationship is something of a salve for real intimacy – one gains a sense of connection but without the same fear of rejection and hurt that would accompany a relationship in the real world.

However, I just want to look at the matter for a moment from what could be described as the other end of the continuum. Occasionally, the individual therapist will have been involved in a primary relationship during her own childhood and/or adolescence in which she experienced a sense of 'merging'. Neville Symington describes such a feeling in his relationship with his mother, whose hypnotic stare he describes as "mesmerising", when he was a youngster and who talked to him as if he were an adult. In the chapter on Carl Jung's life, I drew attention to the young Carl experiencing a sort of 'merging' with his father during his youth. This was significantly fuelled, I think, by the fact that Carl always slept in his father's bed until he left to go to university. Such an experience may result in the individual experiencing an insatiable hunger for a repetition of this merging during adult years. This insatiable need for a close relationship often becomes a feature of an individual's life once the original merged relationship has been lost. I would suggest that Neville Symington lost this quality in his relationship with his mother once she took a lover. My point is perhaps proven by the fact that he admits to being furious and thrown into a sense of 'unbalance' when he was informed of her affair; these feelings led in turn to much unwise decision-making, at Neville's own admission, for a number of years thereafter.

A 'merged' relationship also represents a less-than-optimal attachment experience but one which leaves the individual sometimes compelled to search for a similar experience of 'merging' which will provide some form of satisfaction. The individual then tends to move (unconsciously) into the field of therapy, both as a therapist and as a patient herself, in a drive to gain satisfaction.

I am now moving on to discuss the third theme: the pursuit of a quest. As you perhaps have understood, the second theme of sub-optimal attachment experiences and the third theme are entwined.

The Quest

Many therapists have suffered incredibly during their early years. This may be as a result of occurrences in their families during their formative years; it may be as a result of the political and economic climate into which they were born. For instance, Victor Frankl and Sigmund Freud both suffered the consequences of being part of a Jewish sub-culture, an ethnic minority that has suffered severe discrimination throughout the world over the course of many centuries. However, particularly in Frankl's case, the effects of Hitler's policy of rabid anti-Semitism meant that he suffered severely as a young man, interred as he was for three years in four concentration camps during the Second World War. He not only suffered personally from the absolutely horrific conditions in the camps but also lost his parents, brother and first wife during the war years. He emerged to a different post-war Germany, where traditional ways of life had been riven apart. Few of us undergo such an all-pervasive level of suffering, and it is to his enormous credit that he devised the therapy called logotherapy to help individuals to transcend their personal suffering. No doubt the attempt to find meaning from the tremendous suffering he and others had endured amounted to his personal quest in life. Sigmund Freud's pursuit of psychoanalysis certainly has the hallmarks of a quest, but it is also true that he may have chosen this path because other career paths were not open to him as a Jew. Private practice may have been chosen because promotion was barred to him as a consequence of his ethnicity.

However, others of us who have suffered in less obvious and dire circumstances have a pervasive wish to pursue a personal quest in life. Many of us are engaged in an existential search, at a conscious or partially unconscious level, for a sense of meaning in life, or maybe we are striving to find an answer to some conundrum. We feel that there must be some purpose in life other than simply to survive its vicissitudes. If we are only to encounter the negative effects of suffering, we may well ask the question, as Frankl did: "What is the point of suffering?" Indeed, the title of Viktor Frankl's most famous book is, indeed, *Man's Search for Meaning* (Frankl, 2004).

I think the pursuit of a quest lay beneath the fact that Neville Symington spent a considerable time deciding whether he wanted to devote his life to the service of God before he found his way into the world of psychoanalysis. Carl Jung's life was also defined as a personal quest to understand the workings of the human mind and, in particular, unconscious processes and the meaning of symbolisations. He also retained an interest in the spirit world throughout his life.

I strongly believe that the pursuit of therapy, both on behalf of oneself and as a therapist, to help others to find contentment and peace in their lives represents an answer to one's personal quest. In almost all of the lives that I have studied, there is a persistent and heartfelt search to find a solution to one's own personal quest. The quest that one pursues is closely associated, in my opinion, with the compulsive need for a sense of 'connection'.

'Different From the Norm'?

I find this theme difficult to articulate. I *do* wish to stress that what I am going to say is most definitively not meant pejoratively. Indeed, in contrast, it is meant as a compliment. I firmly believe that most individuals who become therapists with an accompanying sense of vocation are, in actuality, a little different from the majority of people. Of course, it is true to say that we are all unique individuals – no two of us are completely alike; no two of us have borne identical life experiences. Even as siblings, with the same parents and exposure to life events, we view what occurs from differing perspectives. Parents who have twin children will comment to me about the way in which their twins have developed very differently from an early age. Part of this difference is as a result of our unique characteristics and genetic endowment; part is as a result of our different numerical ranking in the structure of our family; part is as a result of the 'myth' that surrounds each child and the role he or she plays in the family drama.

However, the members of our profession that develop a sense of vocation tend to have 'differences' that are similar in nature to one another – though this in itself seems to be a paradox at first glance.

Most of the individuals whose lives I have studied evidence *a resistance to authority*. They do not like to 'be told'; they clearly do not respect individuals who are in power but lack the requisite wisdom to be afforded such power and control. In consequence, I have found examples in their life stories of events in which they have resisted the authority of those they do not respect. For example, Neville Symington found it completely abhorrent to live with Tony Beagle, the priest in the parish to which he was allocated in the East End of London. He felt very strongly that this man lacked wisdom and, furthermore, did not share his own view of God. In fact, Tony Beagle's view of God as a vengeful force unfortunately coincided with that of Neville's father.

Carl Jung had a difficult relationship with Bleuler, his superior at the Burgholzli. At first, he took the role of being the willing pupil, but in time, he made an attempt to usurp the power of his boss, even daring to suggest that Bleuler surrender his role as lecturer at the University to someone who was not in charge at the hospital (namely, to Carl Jung himself). Bleuler replied that he would think about the suggestion but actually ignored the recommendation.

I move on now to consider other ways in which an individual may evidence his or her 'difference', this time with regard to humour. Some individuals tend to display a somewhat wry sense of humour. Take, for example, Patrick Casement's humour (Casement, 2015). He clearly found it comical and highly satisfying that his headmaster had to wait for him – the pupil – to finish translating a passage in Latin! Consciously, he appreciated that his headmaster had stated "Don't hurry!" with a touch of cynicism. Patrick ostensibly took this command at face value and spent some time over his translation. The reader is prone to chuckle to himself when Patrick laughs about the day that he bested his headmaster.

Lastly, I have noted that for most individuals whose lives I have studied, the actual search for a vocation has been a struggle. Most of us have had at least one career, if not more, before embarking upon our training as psychoanalytic therapists and psychoanalysts. We have moved from occupation to occupation until we have, for some reason, found our way (usually) into personal analysis. From this beginning, we have developed a motivation to train as an analyst or psychoanalytic psychotherapist. Again, to use the example of Patrick Casement: he passed through the occupations of brickie's mate, probation officer, family welfare officer, supply teacher and psychoanalytic psychotherapist before finding what he considers to be his true sense of vocation as an analyst. Carl Jung began his employment history as a psychiatrist – so roughly in the arena in which he remained – but he soon grew tired of the way that psychiatrists wanted to make a diagnosis and then simply incarcerated the patients in a secure environment.

Personal Experience of Mental Disturbance

There seems to be an association between the personal hesitation to find a satisfying career and one's own experience of a time of mental disturbance. An analysis of the research has thrown up the likelihood that each individual has, at some time in their life, suffered from a period (sometimes prolonged) of mental illness. I am guided here partially by the writings of Nina Coltart (1993a, 1993b). She perceptively says that it is not a disadvantage to be neurotic, clearly stating that it may well be that the neurotic person is able to understand her patient more fully than the non-neurotic therapist.

I certainly think that one's own experience of mental disturbance means that one appreciates a number of things. Firstly, one appreciates that one is no better than or less vulnerable to the vicissitudes of life than any of our patients who may be undergoing times of mental disturbance when they present in our consulting rooms. This perhaps helps one not to feel omnipotent or grandiose. It helps us to behave with humility. I am certain that it helps one to empathise if one too has undergone the need for help from a mental health professional. Secondly, owning one's experience of a period of time suffering from mental disturbance provides the individual with a fuller understanding of how patients may be feeling at the moment they present in the consulting room. I have said in a previous book on panic disorder and phobia (Fear, 2018) that in my opinion it is impossible to appreciate the sheer debilitating horror of a panic attack unless one has personally suffered the experience. The same argument applies to various other states of mental illness, not least to depression. Who can viscerally identify with the patient feeling that there is no joy to be found in anything in the world unless one too has experienced such a dreadful time in one's own life? I suffered from severe agoraphobia in my early twenties and periods of clinical depression later in life, and I can say now with impunity that in retrospect, I am grateful for these experiences, painful as they were at the time.

It is also true to say, as both Malcolm (1997) and Nina Coltart do, that ours is "an impossible profession" (Coltart, 1993b, p. 2). Just how many of the population would *choose* to spend their hours listening to and analysing others' experience of mental disturbance? It is a fact that psychiatrists – though differing in approach from ourselves as psychotherapists and analysts – are 78% more likely to take their own lives than the general population. This seems to indicate how we as mental health professionals can be affected by what my general practitioner refers to as the "daily portion of poison you imbibe".

I am mindful of Richard Lucas's words in his book, *The Psychotic Wavelength* (2013). He writes that when he was first a psychiatrist, he would experience a dreadful headache as a result of attempting to understand the seeming illogical beliefs of the psychotic individual. I found this statement by Lucas highly reassuring when I worked in a psychiatric hospital during my training. I only worked there one day a week, and each week on that day, I emerged with a splitting headache. I suggest that it was not only my head that was splitting!

I am convinced that the individual life experiences, endured by those whose life stories I have chosen to analyse, have systematically affected their world view. It is to this sixth theme that I now turn.

World View Held by the Subjects of the Research

I have described earlier the four-part typology of world views which I have adopted from the work of Northrop Frye (1957, 1965). The world views are Tragic, Ironic, Romantic and Comic.

It might not surprise you to discover that in all of the analyses, I found evidence of only two world views: namely, the holding of either a Tragic vision or an Ironic vision. When one studies the features of the Tragic vision, one easily perceives that the metatheoretical assumptions of this vision align themselves with the particular individual's adoption of a psychoanalytic theoretical modality. This world view is most likely to be held by an individual who retains a relatively pessimistic view of life, who focusses upon constraints and obstacles rather than seeing life as a series of opportunities. There is a sense of fate; a sense of one's life being concerned with the coming to terms with vicissitudes, focussing on the negatives rather than the positives.

However, for those of us – such as Patrick Casement – who hold a less pessimistic view of life and its vicissitudes, then it appeals to us to continuously indulge in turning the coin over, and looking at the other side in order to find a solution to the problems that one encounters in life. Indeed, my personal mantra is "to make something good out of the bad". I noted that Sigmund Freud, in an imaginary conversation with Brett Kahr (Kahr, 2017, p. 190), makes a similar point to my own: that losing a child represents an all-consuming negative. Freud did, in fact, tragically encounter such an eventuality in his own life – his favoured daughter, Sophia, died very young. I realise that some very courageous individuals reform their life's-purpose by establishing a charity in memory of their lost child.

The world view of Nina Coltart may also have been Ironic. I am sure that she understood the reason for her abhorrence in being left waiting and crafted her life and her interests in consequence. She spoke of it to Molino (Rudnytsky and Preston, 2011) as "a fracture" and commented about the agony of waiting for someone whom she loved and was dependent upon. I am in no doubt that she ended her life because she could not countenance a life in which she would be unable to take care of herself and would need to rely on help from others as a result of the degenerative health problems from which she was suffering.

No-one of a psychoanalytic or psychodynamic persuasion whose life I have studied has seemed to adopt either a Romantic or Comic vision of reality. It seems that Carl Jung had a Romantic bent, which came to the fore when he was planning and executing the building of his family home, Kusnacht, on the lakeside, and again, in later years when he built his fantasy three-tower dwelling (Bollingen) further along the lakeside. It seems to me that the Romantic and Comic visions both deny the negative, the brutality of life that we often behold in our clinical work. I have said for many years that the stories which I am privileged to hear in my consulting room are frequently more strange than the fiction which informs TV programmes or films. They are also frequently infinitely more sad, not least because they are true stories in which individuals have been hurt in ways that do not allow restitution. It is therefore dependent upon the therapist, working alongside the healthy part of the patient's psyche, to help the latter to come to terms with the reality and, hopefully, to help them to take some meaning from the suffering.

The fact that the currency of our work is essentially sad means that this type of work only appeals to individuals who are capable of "holding" (Winnicott, 1965) and "containing" (Bion, 1970, 1984) those patients who make their way to our doors. It is also possible that it is the fact that we deal daily with suffering and pain that trains us, to some extent, to hold a Tragic or Ironic world view. It is one of the occasions when one can argue 'chicken' or 'egg'. We are faced with the central dilemma: which comes first – the perspective on life or the reality of being in receipt of individuals' suffering?

Conclusion

In this chapter, I have discussed the six themes that I have gained from my simultaneous deduction, induction and analysis of the data. These six themes appear time and again in the life stories. Hopefully, your attention will have been drawn to these themes as they announced themselves in the preceding chapters. Whilst trying to tell the life stories in a coherent manner, I have also attempted to highlight the various themes that the analysis rendered from the research. I hope that during your reading of the foregoing chapters, you have appreciated how these six themes in actuality overlap and resonate with one another. I believe that in the identification of these themes, we are able to reach a conclusion regarding the individual's propensity to become in actuality a person who becomes wounded and goes on to find a career in which he or she heals the wounded.

Chapter 12

Reflexivity

The Concept of Reflexivity

Reflexivity is particularly relevant in qualitative social science research (including counselling and psychotherapy research) because the researcher is using qualitative methods to investigate and 'tease out' appropriate concepts, categories and theories from data gathered from their participants/subjects. In the case of the research carried out in the preparation of this book, the 'subjects' have clearly not written their books with the express purpose of providing research data. However, making use of published material, correspondence or diaries is an accepted method of data collection when one engages in qualitative research using grounded theory.

In order to be reflexive, I need to be as aware as possible of the value systems that I hold; I must also consider the biases, assumptions, cultural differences and issues of power and control that I may bring to my own analysis of the data and my discourse position. Reflexivity also involves the need to take account of one's emotional investment in the research and issues of personal identity which may affect the analysis one is endeavouring to carry out. In short, reflexivity involves the researcher trawling through in order to pick out where and if she has been unduly affected by her own set of values and assumptions when carrying out the analysis of the data. Indeed, this may even be so regarding her choice of research material. I guess my choice to look in detail at the concept of the wounded healer is as a result of the subject always interesting me, plus the fact that individuals have often referred to me as one of those healers. As I have indicated, reflexivity is particularly appropriate in qualitative research because one lacks the statistics embedded in quantitative analysis that may tend to support one's hypothesis or, indeed, disprove it. In social science qualitative research, we tend to investigate our subjects' attitudes, value-systems, psychopathologies, characteristic traits and world view. This naturally necessitates that if we are to investigate our subject by seeking out the nuances and subtle indications of which the subject may have no conscious awareness, we need to use qualitative methods of research rather than the 'heavy hammer' approach (employing conscious awareness) of quantitative research (i.e. the use of Likert scales and direct questions in surveys are examples

DOI: 10.4324/9781003316503-13

of this methodology). However, in employing qualitative research, the researcher needs to be keenly aware of her own set of value systems, biases, cultural attitudes, emotional investment and/or financial investment (if any) in order to put her findings in context.

I do believe that the qualitative researcher who practises a career in counselling or psychotherapy is eminently suited to carry out the reflexive process, because there are distinct parallels between the process of reflexivity and the process engaged upon by a therapist in her consulting room for the benefit of her patient. In her clinical work, she will aim to consistently hold in mind an awareness of her own process, of what is and what is not said and of the way in which she is affected by the patient's material and manner of presentation. She will tend to find the processing of these factors quite familiar whilst also simultaneously engaging with her patient's overtly presented material. I am, of course, talking about the therapist's use of the counter-transference, both syntonically as a response to the patient's transference and her own transference that she brings to the consulting room. Such feelings may well emanate from her own experiences in life.

Reflexive Issues Arising From My Research

When I began to consider the value-systems and biases that I had brought to this piece of research, I was immediately struck by the fact that two of the six categories that I devised using grounded theory were actually concepts that I already had an interest in: they are, in fact, subjects about which I have published material in the past. Namely, I am speaking of the effects of personal attachment schemas on the individual's life (Fear, 2017) and, secondly, the concept of visions of reality (Fear and Woolfe, 1996, 1999, 2000). In both cases, I have covered significantly different aspects regarding these concepts in previous publications, but it remains evident to me that my understanding of and familiarity with these concepts may have influenced the ways in which I interpreted the published data. However, even whilst, of course, I now appreciate this to be the case, I also strongly believe that my familiarity with these concepts may have deepened my capacity to analyse the data. Whoever I am and whatever past I may have, I am bound to be influenced by my areas of interest, my specialties, my preoccupations.

However, I feel that I need to focus upon the word 'preoccupation'. I need to evaluate whether these topics preoccupy me to the extent that I see them in every aspect of life. Naturally, as I have always had a keen interest in Bowlby's attachment theory, and thus have used it in my clinical career, nevertheless, I do not believe that I resort to thinking in terms of attachment regarding any data in which I come into contact. For instance, watching Jeremy Corbyn and Theresa May's performances during the election process before the 2017 General Election, I was very aware (upon reflection) that I did not analyse their behaviour in terms of their reported attachment histories. I am certain, however, that I do not see the world purely in terms of attachment. However, when I forced myself to watch the Oprah

Winfrey interview of Prince Harry and Meghan Markle in 2021, I was acutely aware that I did, in fact, try to make some sense of their behaviour by resorting to a consideration of each of their attachment histories as per my psychoanalytic perspective.

So it is accurate to say that the world view that one lives by shares the same metatheoretical assumptions as one's chosen theoretical modality. In consequence, after three decades as a therapist, I admit that I have a certain way of looking at the world. Thus, one could say that I am no more affected by my areas of interest than any other human researcher or, perhaps more accurately stated, than any other analyst. It is only normal for an individual who is prepared to devote a considerable period of time to a project of their own choosing that they feel strongly about the subject matter that they choose to research. Consequently, the argument here is rather along the lines of 'Chicken or egg – which comes first?' It seems to me that any and every researcher must be attuned to their subject matter because it is an area of substantial interest; this may be as a result of previous experience or familiarity with the concepts involved in the study. Thinking of a good friend of mine, Robin, who has just been successful in his doctoral studies, he would not have spent five years of his life studying a subject in which he was not emotionally invested. Similarly, I have become emotionally invested in the concept of woundedness. Consequently, I do recognise an element of possible bias in the concepts and categories that I consider to be important and recurrent regarding the subject of 'woundedness'. I leave it to the reader to judge whether my analysis is worthy of consideration despite my biases.

An area in which I am aware of using my own value system lies in my attitude to boarding at public schools. I am aware that I consciously stiffen at the idea of sending small children – under the age of eleven – to boarding schools unless there is no other logistical choice. My heart goes out to Neville Symington, and I feel both amused and hurt by his referral to Ampleforth College as "Yorkshire's concentration camp". I admit I find it difficult to understand that Patrick Casement believes that his parents made their wisest decision in sending both he, at age seven, and his elder brother to a preparatory boarding school. However, the fact that he commends his parents' choice reveals the extent to which he felt that his family's peripatetic lifestyle in the Royal Navy, especially during the Second World War, seriously undermined his sense of security. I readily admit that my analysis of the dominant attachment schemas of Symington, Casement and Bowlby may well have been partially a result of their parents' choice of schooling method for their children. However, I would guess if you took a straw poll amongst the population, a majority of respondents would agree with me. Certainly, the current trend is to refrain from sending young children to boarding school.

Both Frankl and Freud were of Jewish ethnicity. I am again aware that I have an inbred and conscious feeling of sympathy and empathy towards those individuals with a Jewish heritage. Firstly, my mother worked alongside Jewish individuals as a neophyte teacher in Leeds. Consequently, she raised both my sister and me not to discriminate against individuals of different culture and religious persuasion. Secondly, my husband has worked for three Jewish employers – most of his working life – and their influence has brought us nothing other than fulfilment in our lives and fortunes. Thirdly, two of my friends and my analyst are Jewish. Consequently, I freely admit that I feel a strong sense of repugnance towards the discrimination that both Freud and Frankl experienced during their youths (and, indeed, for the rest of their lives). I keenly appreciate the wounding that emanates from being constantly treated as if you were 'less than'. It could be that I overestimate the effects of discrimination upon Freud and Frankl, but on reflection, I feel that if one reads about Frankl's experience during the Holocaust, I am certain that I have not felt empathy unnecessarily.

I guess that I feel an empathy and a sympathy towards all seven of my subjects as I share a career with them, about which I feel a sense of vocation; maybe I am motivated to answer my own quest. In addition, I believe I have a sub-optimal attachment schema; in truth, I would describe myself as possessing an insecure ambivalent attachment schema. Thus, I believe that I identify with most of these therapists, not least because I hold a Tragic/Ironic vision of reality.

Lastly, I would like to say that I was shocked when I first learned that Nina Coltart took her own life. However, after learning more about her experience as a child and adolescent, I truly believe that it was (Rudnytsky and Preston, 2011, p. 165) both an act of freedom and an act of despair when she took her own life. I cannot verbalise it better than Brendon MacCarthy's words: she was "undone by the pure agony of waiting" (ibid, p. 185). I can understand that she could see no other way forward given her abhorrence of dependency on another, the trauma of waiting for parents who never arrived.

Conclusion

As Liddy Carver (managing editor of *Counselling and Psychotherapy Research*) states in an article in *Therapy Today* that it is important to be transparent and to use one's integrity, rather than to be defensive, during the reflexive process. One needs to be aware of the power asymmetries in the research process and attempt to ameliorate them (Carver, 2017).

Carver goes on to say at the end of her paper that most of us as early-career qualitative researchers are aware of the requirement to be reflexive but that few individuals actually apply the theory in practice. I hope that by including a chapter in which I have tried to recognise and question the biases that I bring to the research, I have at least made an attempt to inject some sense of context and integrity regarding this piece of research. Certainly, I have pointed out a limitation to the research as a consequence of choosing only psychoanalysts or psychoanalytic psychotherapists as subjects. I have stated clearly that my research regarding the premise that psychotherapists may be wounded healers only applies to those individuals of a psychoanalytic or psychodynamic modality. As a trained psychoanalytic psychotherapist myself, it seems unsurprising that I have identified the concepts and categories that appear and reappear in the texts from which I have drawn my findings. After all, it seems to me that our role as analytic therapists is to investigate the relationship between the past and the present, and the categories that I have identified tend to reflect the metatheoretical assumptions of my own world view and choice of theoretic modality.

Chapter 13

Discussion

Findings

In researching and writing this book, I have sought to find out whether psychoanalysts and psychoanalytic psychotherapists fulfil the myth, so often voiced or implied, that they are wounded healers. As in the Greek myth, it is also implied that such individuals have a sense of vocation; consequently, they typically spend decades of their lives healing the wounded. I began my research with a question rather than with a definitive positive or negative hypothesis. Such a question is often employed when the researcher uses grounded theory as the research instrument.

The concept of the wounded healer began in some societies where it was expectable that each village had a shaman. This person had usually suffered an intense physiological and/or psychological breakdown and was now believed to have the power to heal others. In ancient Greek times, this myth focussed upon a centaur named Chiron. I recorded, in an early chapter of the book, how he was physically wounded when his heel was pierced by a poisoned arrow during a night of revelry, and despite the reality that this accident caused him constant pain, the injury determined him to help others to contain and master their wounds. I have also put forward the belief that Christ was the original wounded healer, who suffered physical wounds upon the Cross. Carl Jung was the first therapist to put forward the idea that analysts are indeed wounded healers.

After much consideration, I decided to attempt to analyse whether the life stories of a group of analysts and psychotherapists did or did not exhibit features of 'woundedness'. I chose to undertake secondary research, using published material as the source of data. My research concentrated upon the copious study of a multiple array of various autobiographies and biographies of well-known therapists. My sampling frame was drawn by a literature search of the life stories of therapists. Some were autobiographies, others were biographies, and yet others consisted of the use of theoretical texts which contained some reference to their own life. My intuition proved to be correct: analytic therapists tend to be exceedingly private individuals and, in consequence, have not felt inclined to write their autobiographies. I particularly commend the decisions of Neville Symington, Patrick

DOI: 10.4324/9781003316503-14

Casement and Viktor Frankl, who each wrote a number of books concerning their own path through life. I am one among many, I am sure, that have found the accounts of their life stories exceptionally absorbing, illuminating, compulsive reading.

Prior to beginning the research, I made the decision to use grounded theory as my research tool. Glaser and Strauss, and later Corbin, were all instrumental in developing this method of qualitative research during the 1960s, when quantitative research was the favoured modality of enquiry. Essentially, research using grounded theory involves a simultaneous process of deduction, induction and analysis of one's data. The researcher begins the research with a question or possibly just with a particular subject matter in mind rather than employing the definitive hypotheses used in quantitative research. The researcher studies the texts – be they old letters, books, original documents or ephemera – and attempts to identify and then code the ideas that she repeatedly finds in the first text. As the name implies, the research process is grounded in the actual texts. The researcher then takes a second text and searches out any new ideas. She also notes down if and when the same ideas appear in the second text. If the idea does not repeat in subsequent texts, she then discards that concept. She gives a code (usually a letter) to each repeating idea. In this way, the researcher develops a list of codes. Her process of deduction and analysis continues as she begins to find that some of the codes are linked by their subject matter to one another. Realising this, she develops a word or phrase that encompasses these related ideas. These are known as categories. She deduces that some of the codes share the same conceptual underpinnings. For example, the researcher may at first have noted down a code for 'mother died when individual was adolescent', 'cried copiously when left home to go to boarding school', 'only found security in relationship with grandmother'. The term 'attachment difficulties' forms an umbrella term for all of these related ideas. Another text might reveal the following codes: 'parents killed in train crash when child only eleven years of age', 'mother not emotionally available because of depression when he was adolescent', 'father arranged for the evacuation of his family from Portugal to USA'. The researcher then deduces that all of these ideas are linked and can be categorised as 'a traumatological event during childhood'. See here that one uses a phrase to name this category. By studying these categories (which I have chosen to call 'themes'; cf. Chapter 11), the researcher may be able to deduce a new theory which marries the themes together and puts forward an answer to the question she posed at the inception of the research.

In the case of the research into the myth of the 'wounded healer', I believe that the process has enabled me to analyse various aspects of the research question. Firstly, the evidence that I gathered was such that it seems that it is highly likely that many of our psychoanalytic therapists can be accurately described as wounded healers because they have suffered two of the themes (attachment difficulties and a traumatic event) during their childhood or early adult life. My analysis evidences that these two themes occur repeatedly, often presenting in a linked format in the subjects' life stories: namely, they have all suffered from a distinctive trauma during their early years, and as a result of the trauma, coupled with the dynamics within their family of origin, they have developed a sub-optimal attachment schema. The research of Van Ijzendoorn and Sagi-Schwartz (2008) accurately shows that a third of the population in the Western world suffers from a sub-optimal attachment schema; namely, the individuals have adopted an insecure avoidant or insecure ambivalent attachment schema. However, it is certainly untrue that all such people find their way into the profession of psychotherapist or counsellor. However, I think it is credible that many such individuals with sub-optimal attachment patterns do, indeed, establish a career for themselves in the helping professions, be that as a care assistant in a nursing home or as a nurse, doctor, social worker or teacher (to name just a few of the caring professions).

You will no doubt have noticed that contrary to the myth of the illustrious centaur, the wounds these real-life individuals have suffered have been psychological and emotional in origin rather than physical. It seems to me, during my thirty years as a psychotherapist, that the number of therapists who suffer from physical disability are few and far between.

I gradually deduced that another theme occurred repeatedly in my research into the lives of the therapists that I studied. I feel it is perhaps pertinent that most of the subjects in my research had suffered from a sustained period of mental disturbance. Maybe one can surmise that an individual feels more inclined to help others in psychological ill health if he or she has suffered in this way at some time. I am reminded of Nina Coltart's statement that the neurotic therapist may well be equipped to do a better job than the therapists without a neurosis (Rudnytsky and Preston, 2011). Perhaps it could be said that he or she can empathise more fully because of his or her own experience? It may also be true that some therapists tend to be grateful for the help they received at a time of need and thus feel an urge to 'repay' their debt. This has certainly been true in my own life. Or in Patrick Casement's case (who distinctly felt his treatment was ineffective), did he perhaps want to provide a better experience for others than he unfortunately endured?

The fourth theme that my analysis of the life stories evidenced sounds rather strange: each of the individuals seemed 'different from the norm' in some subtle way. I surmise that this 'difference' constitutes another important factor in one's journey into a career as a therapist as opposed to other careers in the helping professions. As a practical example of this 'difference', I noted that quite a number of subjects displayed considerable resistance to authority figures and disliked 'being told'. Patrick Casement's experience at school is paradigmatic of this. I know that I too have always experienced a resistance to authority, particularly if I believe that those in authority lack the wisdom that their role ought to encompass. It is therefore not surprising, at a pragmatic level, that individuals who feel thus find their way into a profession where they are not at the continual beck and call of a boss. Thus, I contend that such individuals unconsciously seek out a profession in which they carry out their primary role in one-to-one communication with their patients, without the interference of a person in authority in the same room. Naturally, in order to work ethically, we as therapists expect to participate in the process of supervision, but it remains a fact that our supervisors are not actually physically present in the room whilst we engage with our patients. The verbatim accounts of sessions that one is called to produce during training mean that the therapist is subject to the role of very direct authority figures. I admit that I found such an intensive method of supervision very difficult to countenance during my training, yet if I had my time again, I would not miss the experience, because through it, I learned so much about technique and counter-transference issues that I otherwise may not have acquired.

The fifth theme that I deduced in the process of analysis concerned the sense of each person being driven to search for, then find and satisfy, a 'quest' in life. In analysing most of the subjects' lives, I found that each of them proceeded during their youth and young adult years to search for a career that provided the satisfaction that they were, indeed, employed in a meaningful quest. Perhaps this is often recognised as the search for a vocation: the struggle to answer an overpowering need to find a career which helps the individual to make sense of the world. To satisfy this feeling, I would suggest one needs to find a career about which one has an abiding passion. Thus, we see that many of my subjects changed career, sometimes – like Patrick Casement and Neville Symington – a number of times before they settled on a career which answered their quest. Nina Coltart trained first as a doctor in order, she realised later, to identify with her father. My own experience in terms of career is mirrored in this theme, too. I have worked in banking, as a librarian, as a market researcher and a lecturer and tutor before I settled on my thirty-year career as a psychoanalytic psychotherapist. Whilst I enjoyed some of the other roles (and others not at all!), I never achieved a sense of deep satisfaction and contentment until I embarked upon my training as a counsellor with Relate in 1990. I was immediately hooked and fascinated by the process of discovering what makes each individual tick whilst also helping the client to recover. I had indeed been helped myself in my early adult life by a psychologist when I suffered from agoraphobia.

The final, sixth theme is that of the vision of reality or world view (*weltanschauung*) held by each of the subjects that I studied in the literature. I think it is fitting that this should comprise the last theme to be discussed, as I believe that this constitutes one of the most significant findings of the research. My analysis showed that all of the research subjects hold/held either an Ironic vision or a Tragic vision of reality or maybe even a mixture of the two. The essence of a Tragic vision lies in the belief that some life experiences are irredeemable and that not all can be remedied, changed or forgotten. I believe that the subjects of the research all suffered during childhood or early adult years from life events which left a mark upon them that they found to be indelible. To continue the metaphor, they could not erase its effects. As an example, I will talk briefly about the two Jewish therapists, Sigmund Freud and Viktor Frankl. The overt level of abhorrent discrimination that they suffered as children, adolescents and adults was to have a permanent effect upon their developing personalities and attitude to life. This may well explain one of the foremost unconscious motivations that led Freud to place such precedence upon childhood experience and its lasting effect upon the individual. Freud is known to have referred to some of his patients as "rabble" (cf. Chapter 7). I think that this represents a reflection of how, deep down, he felt that many patients could not be cured and, indeed, lacked the intellectual and emotional capacity and the commitment to come to terms with their life experiences. Indeed, he made the point numerous times that 'cure' was not the aim of psychoanalysis – the aim, indeed, was rather to help the patient to come to terms with life's vicissitudes. To exchange neurosis for common unhappiness! Without doubt this statement accurately reflects the essence of the Tragic vision of reality!

In contrast, Viktor Frankl suffered the appalling experience in early adulthood of incarceration in prison camps during Hitler's regime, in addition to the institutional racial discrimination that both he and Freud suffered. Nevertheless, regardless of this dire experience, Frankl was determined to surmount its negative effects and to make something positive from it. He had written a manuscript (which was extracted from his own coat in the first camp he entered by jeering officials who refused his request to retain it) before he was interred for three years. Whilst in the camps, he wrote notes for the book on scraps of paper garnered for him by fellow prisoners. Undoubtedly, the intended publication of this book enabled him to transcend his suffering and provided him with the motivation to stay alive. This document outlined the way in which man needs to find salvation by searching for and finding a meaning for his suffering i.e. the need to transcend his suffering. It is worth noting that Frankl's actual experience of emotional, physical and psychological suffering in the camps, plus the deaths of both his parents, his brother and his first wife, did not deter him from his determination to transcend his own suffering. This led to the publication in German in 1946 of his seminal text, *Man's Search for Meaning* (Frankl, 2004). The fact that Frankl was capable of taking this optimistic stance on life provides us with sufficient evidence in itself that he held an Ironic vision of reality rather than a Tragic vision. He was a living example of how one can strive to take the positive from the negative.

In conclusion concerning the theme of world views, my analysis showed that the individuals studied followed one of two visions of reality: namely, they attest to a Tragic or an Ironic world view. Whilst the Tragic vision is indeed more pessimistic than the Ironic vision – the latter often takes an optimistic stance that the individual is capable of finding something positive to gain from life's traumas – both of these visions of reality are on the pessimistic end of the optimistic–pessimistic continuum. This is in direct contrast to the optimistic stance taken by the Romantic and Comic visions of reality. None of the subjects in the research evidence either a dominant Romantic or Comic vision. There is seen to be a proclivity to focus on constraints in life rather than opportunities. In the Ironic world view, the locus of control is internal to the individual, whereas in the Tragic world view, the locus of control is felt to be external to the individual. It is only possible for the individual to come to terms with life's misfortunes; one cannot change them or nullify them.

The finding that all the subjects of the research hold/held either a Tragic or Ironic vision is, in fact, borne out by the evidence from previous research into the world views of therapists of differing modalities. The research (Messer and Winokur, 1984; Shafer, 1976; Fear and Woolfe, 1996, 1999, 2000) evidences that those therapists of a psychoanalytic or psychodynamic modality tend towards a Tragic vision and those of an eclectic or integrative modality tend towards an Ironic vision of reality. I contend that those individuals who have been 'wounded' in childhood are far more likely to feel drawn towards a psychoanalytic modality or towards an integrative form of psychodynamics as a result of negative experiences in life and a tendency to see life in terms of constraints rather than opportunities. The integrative psychodynamic models to which I refer include therapeutic modalities such as cognitive analytic therapy (CAT) (Ryle and Kerr, 2002) or brief psychodynamic models that incorporate behavioural techniques such as cyclical psychodynamics (Wachtel and McKinney, 1992).

The first three themes outlined provide us with evidence that the research subjects are/were all 'wounded' as a result of life events in childhood or early adult life. The fourth, fifth and sixth themes enable one to analyse why these individuals found their way into a career in which they devote their time to healing the wounded rather than taking another career within the helping professions.

It seems to me that there is evidence to suggest that these six themes are the *sine qua non* to becoming not only a wounded person but also a person who chooses to spend her or his life *healing the wounded*.

Does the Theory Drawn From the Research Indicate Something More?

The research findings indicate that it is accurate to say that psychoanalytic psychotherapists and psychoanalysts can be described by the phrase 'wounded healers'. Next, I think there is a need to address how this reality affects our patients and also ourselves as therapists. Would it be accurate to say that as therapists suffering from our own wounds, we enter into this profession purposefully and consciously to enlarge our knowledge about woundedness and use the hours we spend as therapists for our own therapeutic purposes? I have stated in the introduction that if this is so, this seems to me to be something that is intrinsically unethical. We should not spend our time helping others with the covert yet conscious intention of helping ourselves. I would contend that even well-known altruists derive a strong sense of satisfaction from their beneficence. It is true that altruism has its own satisfactions.

Is it not a reality that we are both unconsciously and consciously drawn to those aspects of life that interest and fascinate us most? Does it therefore not follow that we may well be drawn to the profession of psychotherapy as a result of our own devouring interest in pathologies caused by woundedness?

John Klauber, Neville Symington's training analyst, made the point that the patient and analyst have a peculiar but very definite relationship. Both have a need for the other: the patient to use the analyst as a receptacle for his feelings, the therapist to crystallise his thoughts on intimate human problems (Klauber in Symington, 2011, p. 297). I found that Klauber eloquently and precisely mirrored my own thoughts. I am delighted that someone else has voiced these beliefs. As therapists, we do indeed use our patients in order to develop our ideas about life, perhaps because we find this subject so fascinating. However, I also believe that we use (but do not exploit) our patients to satisfy a distinct urge to find and secure a way of feeling connected to another human being in an intimate way. I have said elsewhere that I feel that as a result of our attachment histories – dependent on either a lack or surfeit of 'connectedness' – we unconsciously search to satisfy this urge in our professional lives. Notwithstanding this statement, I find no evidence from the research that any individuals pursue a career as a psychotherapist purely to satisfy their own emotional needs. I remain pleased – and relieved – with this seminal finding. However, I would wish to qualify this. I think it is highly likely that those of us who are wounded feel drawn to help those who themselves are wounded. It seems to me that our own 'woundedness' *sensitises* us to the wounds of others. By this, I mean that as a consequence of our own wounds, we more readily empathise and are drawn to the wounds of others. It may well be that by helping others and learning about the complex nature of woundedness, we benefit from this career choice by creating a salve for our own wounds. We may also gain in knowledge and achieve a greater understanding about our own emotional process. In this way, it could be argued that *we gain vicariously* by helping others.

Finally, I want to make two more points regarding our choice of career as psychotherapists. In the process of learning to be therapists (especially those of us who have undergone a psychoanalytic training), we are taught to refrain from disclosing information about ourselves in the consulting room. I believe that this may well suit a lot of individual therapists who have endured difficult attachment experiences. If the individual therapist suffers from an insecure ambivalent or insecure avoidant attachment schema, then she or he may well have *an inclination to avoid any personal vulnerability*. Nina Coltart's correspondence with her friends evidenced this very well – she is said to rarely have revealed anything about herself. Thus, we could say that the rule of abstinence serves us well with regard to our avoidance of obvious causes of distress. However, we must be able to withstand the effect in our counter-transference; this can be deeply disturbing at times. Also, I am certain that we have all experienced the effect of a patient unconsciously using a process of projective identification in order to displace his feelings onto us.

It seems to me also that we may inadvertently use our role to *compensate ourselves* for the difficulties which reside in us emotionally as a result of our dominant attachment schema. Let me explain. If we searched for but could not achieve a meaningful connection in our initial primary attachment, then I suggest that we unconsciously seek to fulfil this urge to *connect at a deep level* by spending our hours in intense discussions with our patients. Our working life thus provides us with a sense of connection that we may have lacked until the time we became therapists. In this way, we are helped to compensate for what was lacking in our childhood experience of relationships. The converse is also true, I feel – if, on the other hand, our initial attachment experience included a sense of merging with our attachment object. We may have then experienced a deep sense of connection, and we may hunger to replicate this experience in later life. I do not believe that decisions regarding our choice of career are made consciously with this in mind, but I think it explains why and how we satisfy the search for a quest that may have dominated our life until we make this career choice. For those who have experienced a merged relationship in childhood or adolescence, I do believe that there is a significant danger in that one can become over-involved with patients in a long-term therapy.

Recommendations for Further Research

There remain a number of points to make regarding this research, and I would also like to include recommendations for further research.

This research has been carried out using the life stories of a number of psychoanalytic psychotherapists and psychoanalysts. My conclusions have also been influenced by my own early life and the satisfaction that I have derived from a long and satisfying career as a psychoanalytic psychotherapist, albeit one who has gradually, over a process of years, developed her own personal integrative model of therapy (cf. Fear, 2017).

Firstly, for reasons of time constraints and availability of secondary data, my research sample has been undeniably small in number. However, I have attempted to ameliorate this by using a number of books to research the lives of each person. Therefore, I think this research may prompt others to study this subject using different research methods. I believe that it may be valuable if a research student in the future were to use semi-structured interviewing of proficient psychotherapists (not trainees) to discover their world views and motivations in choosing a career as therapists. This was discounted by me as a possible mode of enquiry owing to lack of availability of such a sampling frame. There is, also, as I suggested earlier in the introduction, the difficulty of whether individual therapists have actually given enough conscious thought to their motivations to become a psychotherapist and whether they are capable of articulating their understanding in a meaningful way. The researcher would also have to contend with the problem of whether individuals are prepared to share intimate details or, indeed, are willing to talk about painful areas of their lives. The use of focus groups could also be an avenue open to further research, and one may be able to discover true motivations of therapists by the intensive and confidential methods employed in this manner of research. I believe that the study in this text sets the scene for further research for those interested in this subject. There is certainly a dearth of literature on the subject at the present time.

I also feel a need to express that I unfortunately must limit the application of my findings to those of us who have chosen to work with our patients in a psychoanalytic/psychodynamic modality. Whilst I think it is eminently possible that the findings do apply to many of us in the field of eclectic or integrative modalities of counselling or, indeed, in other caring professions, I equally think that the findings may well not be applicable to those therapists who follow cognitive-behavioural (CBT) or humanistic modalities. Certainly, research evidences that therapists of such modalities tend to hold a Comic or Romantic vision of reality (Messer and Winokur, 1984). CBT counsellors and therapists do not give as much priority to early life events, and they may well emphasise (both in their personal world view and their work with patients) the opportunities in life rather than the constraints which confront the individual.

References

Ainsworth, M.D., Blehar, M.C., Waters, E., & Wall, S. (1978). *Patterns of Attachment: A Psychological Study of the Strange Situation*. Hillsdale, NJ: Erlbaum.

Bair, D. (2004). *Jung: A Biography*. London: Little, Brown.

Balint, M. (1968). *The Basic Fault: Therapeutic Aspects of Regression*. London: Routledge.

Bion, W. (1970). *Attention and Interpretation*. London: Tavistock.

Bion, W. (1984). *Learning from Experience*. London: Karnac.

Bowlby, J. (1940). The influence of the environment in the development of the neuroses and neurotic character. *International Journal of Psycho-Analysis, 21*: 154–178.

Bowlby, J. (1944). Forty-four juvenile thieves: Their characters and home life. *International Journal of Psychoanalysis, 25*: 1–57 and 107–228.

Bowlby, J. (1979). *The Making and Breaking of Affectional Bonds*. London: Hogarth.

Bowlby, J. (1988). *A Secure Base: Clinical Applications of Attachment Theory*. London: Routledge.

Bowlby, J., & Robertson, J. (1952a). A two-year-old goes to hospital: A scientific film. *Proceedings of the Royal Society of Medicine, 46*: 425–427.

Carotenuto, A. (1982). *A Secret Symmetry: Sabina Spielrein between Jung and Freud*, p. 93. New York: Pantheon Books.

Carver, L. (2017). *Therapy Today*: 2017–09–15.

Casement, P. (1985). *On Learning from the Patient*, pp. 57–71. London: Tavistock.

Casement, P. (1990). *Further Learning from the Patient*. London: Routledge.

Casement, P. (2006). *Learning from Life: Becoming a Psychoanalyst*. London: Routledge.

Casement, P. (2015). *Growing Up? A Journey with Laughter*. London: Karnac.

Charmaz, K. (2006). *Constructing Grounded Theory*. Thousand Oaks, CA: Sage.

Clay, C. (2016). *Labyrinths*. London: William Collins.

Coltart, N. (1986). Slouching towards Bethlehem . . . or thinking the unthinkable in psychoanalysis. In: N. Coltart (ed.) *Slouching Towards Bethlehem . . . . . . and Further Psychoanalytic Explorations*, pp. 1–14. London: Free Association Books.

Coltart, N. (1993a). *How to Survive as a Psychotherapist*, p. 101. London: Sheldon Press.

Coltart, N. (1993b). *Slouching Towards Bethlehem . . . . . . and Further Psychoanalytic Explorations*. London: Free Association Books.

Coltart, N. (1996a). *The Baby and the Bathwater*. London: Karnac.

Coltart, N. (1996b). Two's company, three's a crowd. In: *The Baby and the Bathwater*, pp. 41–56. London: Karnac.

Cooper, J. (2016). *Mount*. London: Penguin Random House.

Dunne, C. (2015). *Carl Jung: Wounded Healer of the Soul*. London: Watkins.

Eliade, M. (1972). *Shamanism Archaic Techniques of Ecstasy*. Princeton, NJ: Princeton University Press.

Fear, R.M. (2004). One training voice: Reflecting on the echoes. In: V. Davies, G. Alred, K. Hunt, & G. Davies (eds.) *Experiences of Counsellor Training*, pp. 108–124. Basingstoke: Palgrave MacMillan.

Fear, R.M. (2016). *The Oedipus Complex Solutions or Resolutions?* London: Karnac.

Fear, R.M. (2017). *Attachment Theory: Working Towards Learned Security*. London: Karnac.

Fear, R.M. (2018). *Systematic Desensitization for Panic and Phobia*. London: Karnac.

Fear, R.M., & Woolfe, R. (1996). Searching for integration in counselling practice. *British Journal of Guidance and Counselling*, *24*(3): 399–411.

Fear, R.M., & Woolfe, R. (1999). The personal and the professional development of the counsellor: The relationship between personal philosophy and theoretical orientation. *Counselling Psychology Quarterly*, *12*(3): 253–262.

Fear, R.M. & Woolfe, R. (2000). The personal, the professional and the basis of integrative practice. In: S. Palmer & R. Woolfe (eds.) *Integrative and Eclectic Counselling and Psychotherapy*, pp. 329–340. London: Sage.

Ferenczi, S. (1932). *The Clinical Diary of Sandor Ferenczi* (M. Balint, M. Zarday, & P. Jackson, Trans., & J. Dupont, eds.), pp. 185–186. Cambridge, MA: Harvard University Press.

Frankl, V. (2000). *Viktor Frankl Recollections: An Autobiography*. London: Basic Books.

Frankl, V. (2004). *Man's Search for Meaning*. London: Random House Group.

Freud, S. (1900). The interpretation of dreams. *S.E.*, *5*. London: Hogarth.

Freud, S. (1901a). *Three Essays on the Theory of Sexuality. (1949)*, pp. 135–230. London: Hogarth.

Freud, S. (1901b). The psychopathology of everyday life *S.E.*, *6*. London: Hogarth.

Freud, S. (1905). Jokes and their relation to the unconscious. *S.E.*, *8*. London: Hogarth.

Freud, S. (1913). On beginning the treatment: (Further recommendations on the technique of psychoanalysis I). *S.E.*, *12*: 123–144. London: Hogarth.

Freud, S. (1914). Remembering, repeating and working through (Further recommendations on the technique of psycho-analysis II). *S.E.*, *12*: 145–156. London: Hogarth.

Freud, S. (1927). Postscript to the question of lay analysis. *S.E.*, *20*: 251–258. London: Hogarth.

Freud, S. (1932–6). New introductory lectures on psychoanalysis and other works. *S.E.*, *2*. London: Hogarth.

Freud, S. (1937). Trans. Strachey, J. Analysis terminable and interminable. *International Journal of Psychoanalysis*, *18*: 373–405.

Freud, S. (1950 [1892–1899]). Extracts from the Fliess papers, Letter 7. *S.E.*, *1*: 265. London: Hogarth.

Freud, S. (1950 [1892–1899]). Extracts from the Fliess Papers. *S.E.*, *1*: 177–282. London: Hogarth.

Freud, S., & Breuer, J. (1895). Studies on hysteria. *S.E.*, *20*. London: Hogarth.

Frye, N. (1957). *Anatomy of Criticism*. Princeton, NJ: Princeton University Press.

Frye, N. (1965). *A Natural Perspective: The Development of Shakespearean Comedy and Romance*. New York: Columbia University Press.

Glaser, A. (1967). *Awareness of Dying*. New York: Aldine de Gruyter.

Glaser, A., & Strauss, J. (1967). *The Discovery of Grounded Theory: Strategies for Qualitative Research*. New York: Aldine de Gruyter.

Green, A. (1983). *Narcissisme de Vie. Narcissisme de Mort*. Paris: Editions de Minuet.

Harding Davies, V., Alred, G., Hunt, K., & Davies, G. (eds.) (2004). *Experiences of Counsellor Training: Challenges, Surprises and Change*. Basingstoke: Palgrave Macmillan.

Holmes, J. (1993). *John Bowlby and Attachment Theory*. London: Routledge.

Jones, E. (1953, 1955, 1957). *Sigmund Freud: Life and Work*, 3 volumes. London: Hogarth.

Jung, C.G., & Jaffe, A. (2019). *Memories, Dreams, Reflections*. London: Collins.

Kahr, B. (2017). *Coffee with Freud*, p. 190. London: Karnac.

Kohut, H. (1971). *The Analysis of the Self*. New York: International Universities Press.

Kohut, H. (1977). *The Restoration of the Self*. New York: International Universities Press.

Kohut, H. (1984). *How Does Analysis Cure?* Chicago: Chicago University Press.

Lorenz, K. (1937). The companion in the bird's world. *The Auk, 54*(1): 245–273.

Lucas, R. (2013). *The Psychotic Wavelength: A Psychoanalytic Perspective for Psychiatry*. London: Routledge.

Main, M., & Goldwyn, R. (1984). Predicting rejection of her infant from mother's representation of her own experience: Implications for the abused-abuser intergenerational cycle. *International Journal of Child Abuse and Neglect, 8*: 203–217.

Main, M., & Solomon, J. (1990). Procedures for identifying infants as disorganised/disorientated during the Ainsworth Strange Situation. In: M.T. Greenberg, D. Cicchetti, & E.M. Cummings (eds.) *Attachment in the Pre-School Years*. Chicago, IL: University of Chicago Press.

Malcolm, J. (1997). *Psychoanalysis: The Impossible Profession*. London: Granta.

McAdams, D.P. (1993). *The Stories We Live By*. London: Sage.

McLeod, J. (1993). *Doing Counselling Research*. London: Sage.

McGuire, W. (ed.). (1974). Trans. R. Mannheim & R.F.C. Hull. The Freud/Jung Letters. 1908–1939. In: C. Clay (ed.) *Labyrinths*, p. 210. London: William Collins.

Messer, S.B., & Winokur, M. (1980). Some limits to the integration of psychoanalytic and behaviour therapy. *American Psychologist*: 817–827.

Messer, S.B., & Winokur, M. (1984). Ways of knowing and visions of reality in psychoanalytic therapy and behavior therapy. In: H. Arkowitz & S.B. Messer (eds.) *Psychoanalytic Therapy and Behavior Therapy: Is Integration Possible?* New York: Plenum.

Messer, S.B., & Winokur, M. (1986). Eclecticism and the shifting visions of reality in three systems of psychotherapy. *International Journal of Eclectic Psychotherapy*: 115–112.

Molino, A. (1997). For Nina Coltart: In memoriam, or calling a thing by its name. In: P. Rudnytsky & G. Preston (eds.) *Her Hour Come Round at Last: A Garland for Nina Coltart*, pp. 187–195. London: Karnac.

Phillips, A. (2014). *Becoming Freud: The Making of a Psychoanalyst*. New Haven: Yale University Press.

Powers, A. (2016). *Forced Endings in Psychotherapy and Psychoanalysis: Attachment and Loss in Retirement*. Abingdon: Routledge.

Rudnytsky, P.L., & Preston, G. (2011). *Her Hour Come Round at Last: A Garland for Nina Coltart*. London: Karnac.

Ruitenbeck, H.M. (1973). *Freud as We Knew Him*, p. 141. Detroit: Wayne University Press.

Ryle, A., & Kerr, I.B. (2002). *Introducing Cognitive Analytic Therapy*. Chichester: John Wiley.

Shafer, R. (1976). *A New Language for Psychoanalysis*. New Haven: Yale University Press.

Shostrum, E. (1964). *Three Approaches to Psychotherapy* (Film). Corona Del Mar, CA: Psychological and Educational Films.

Stern, D. (1985). *The Interpersonal World of the Infant*. New York: Basic Books.

Stevens, A. (1994). *On Jung*, p. 110. Princeton, NJ: Princeton University Press.

Stolorow, R.D., Brandchaft, B., & Atwood, G.E. (1983). Self-psychology – a structural psychology. In: J. Lichtenberg & S. Kaplan (eds.) *Reflections of Self-Psychology*, pp. 287–296. Hillsdale, NJ: Princeton University Press.

Stolorow, R.D., Brandchaft, B., & Atwood, G.E. (1995). *Psychoanalytic Treatment: An Intersubjective Approach*. London: Routledge.

Strauss, J., & Corbin, J. (1990). *Basics of Qualitative Research: Grounded Theory Procedures and Techniques*. Newbury Park, CA: Sage.

Sutherland, J. (1991). Reminiscences of John Bowlby. *Tavistock Gazette*.

Symington, N. (1996). *The Making of a Psychotherapist*. London: Karnac.

Symington, N. (2016). *A Different Path: An Emotional Autobiography*. London: Karnac.

Thornton, E.M. (1984). The Freudian Fallacy. In: R. Webster (ed.) *Why Freud Was Wrong*, p. 22. London: Harper Collins.

Van Ijzendoorn, M.H., & Kroonenberg, P.M. (1988). Cross-cultural patterns of attachment: A Meta-Analysis of the Strange Situation. *Child Development*: 147–156.

Van Ijzendoorn, M.H., & Sagi-Schwartz, A. (2008). Cross-cultural patterns of attachment: Universal and contextual dimensions. In: J. Cassidy & P. Shaver (eds.) *Handbook of Attachment: Theory, Research, and Clinical Applications*, pp. 880–905. New York: Guilford.

Wachtel, P.L., & McKinney, M.K. (1992). Cyclical psychodynamics and integrative psychodynamic therapy. In: J.C. Norcross & M.R. Goldfried (eds.) *Handbook of Psychotherapy Integration*, pp. 335–370. New York: Basic Books.

Webster, R. (1995). *Why Freud Was Wrong*. London: Harper Collins.

Weiss, E. (1991). Sigmund Freud as a consultant. In: A. Koellreuter (ed.) *What Is This Professor Freud Like?* p. 94. London: Karnac.

White, H. (1973). Metahistory. In: S.B. Messer & M. Winokur (eds.) Eclecticism and the Shifting Visions of Reality in Three Systems of Psychotherapy. *International Journal of Eclectic Psychotherapy*: 116.

Winnicott, D.W. (1965). *The Maturational Processes and the Facilitating Environment*. London: Karnac.

Zepf, S., & Zepf, F.D. (2016). *Oedipus and the Oedipus Complex*. London: Routledge.

Index